Laying Foundations

Phase II

Growing Spiritually

Pocket Principles®
and Guided Discussions

For Leaders

NOTE: In an effort to recognize that both men and women are co-heirs of God's grace, we have chosen to use alternating gender pronouns in this document. However, we do recognize and embrace gender-specific roles in Scripture.

Development Team:
Bob Dukes
Margaret Garner
Jack Larson
Margo Theivagt

Writing Team:
Buddy Eades
Nancy Higgins
Jack Larson
Jon Long

Publishing Team:
Nila Duffitt
Buddy Eades
Margaret Garner
David Parfitt

Design by Cristina van de Hoeve
doodlingdesigner.com

A Welcome from WDA's President
Worldwide Discipleship Association, Inc.

Hello Friend!

Let me congratulate you on your decision to learn more about Jesus Christ and what it means to follow Him. There is nothing more important or more rewarding than the decision to follow Him and then to grow as a Christian.

These studies will help you get started on your journey with Christ or encourage and instruct you if you are already on this exciting journey. We in WDA want to help you grow and become all you can be in Christ Jesus!

Because you have chosen to lead, we want to do all we can to support you. In addition to the materials provided in this workbook, we would like to also offer you a free download of the Teaching Outlines for *Growing Spiritually*.
http://www.disciplebuilding.org/materials/
growing-spiritually-teaching-outlines-free-download

My prayer and confident belief is that "he who began a good work in you will carry it on to completion until the day of Christ Jesus" (Philippians 1:6) so that He is able "to present you before his glorious presence without fault and with great joy." (Jude 1:24) To Him be glory and praise!

May God richly bless you as you strive to grow in Him.

Bob Dukes
President, Worldwide Discipleship Association
Fayetteville, GA 30214

Growing Spiritually
Table of Contents: Leader

Leader's Instructions
For Using Pocket Principles®

What is a Pocket Principle™? Each Pocket Principle™ is a brief essay that focuses on a single topic necessary to the growth and maturity of a believer.

The 10 Pocket Principles®, about *Growing Spiritually*, help the disciple understand how Christian growth occurs, God's role (including the Holy Spirit) and man's role in spiritual growth, dimensions of spiritual growth and God's plan for believers.

Using Pocket Principles® in a Guided Discussion (small group) format:

You will notice that each Pocket Principle™ has a corresponding Guided Discussion. Because the students who are studying *Growing Spiritually* are usually less mature believers, our suggestion is that they **not be required** to read the Pocket Principles® before coming to the Guided Discussion or after the Discussion. At this point in their maturity, it is best that they be given no work to do outside of the group discussion. (For more information about this, go to our website at www.disciplebuilding.org/about/phases-of-christian-growth/2.) Of course, you can mention the purpose of the Pocket Principles® and **invite** students to read them. The content of the Pocket Principles® will reinforce truth learned in the group discussion. Also, if a group member misses a meeting, he can read the corresponding Pocket Principle™ to review the information missed.

Using Bible Readings:

The booklet entitled *Bible Readings for Devotional Use* is for the student to use in her devotional times. (This is the same booklet used in Cornerstone *Knowing God* and *Understanding People*.) The Bible readings (for a year) focus on the books of *John, Colossians, I John, Genesis, Exodus, Philippians, Jonah* and some of the *Psalms*. These books have been chosen because they emphasize many of the topics studied in the Cornerstone series. If the student has already begun using the *Bible Readings*, she should continue.

Using Pocket Principles® in a Life Coaching (one-one) format:

Pocket Principles® can also be used effectively in an interactive one-one relationship. However, in this arrangement we suggest that the Life Coach (discipler) ask the student to read the Pocket Principle™ beforehand so the material can be discussed during the one-one appointment. All the dynamics mentioned above still apply and the Life Coach needs to tailor expectations to the maturity of the student. To facilitate interaction, the material contained in the corresponding Guided Discussion for Leaders will help a Life Coach prepare for the appointment. (For more information about preparing for a Life Coaching appointment, please consult the *Life Coaching Manual* at www.disciplebuilding.org/product-category/life-coaching.)

Leader's Instructions
For Using Guided Discussions

The 10 Guided Discussions, about *Growing Spiritually*, help the disciple understand how Christian growth occurs, the roles of God (including the Holy Spirit) and believers in spiritual growth, the dimensions of spiritual growth and God's plan for believers.

Guided Discussions for small groups play an important role in the growth of a believer with the **major goal being interaction around Scripture**. The goal of disciple building is not just knowledge, but Christlikeness in character and conduct. Therefore, **application is essential**. (Sections "Looking At Real Life" and "Looking at My Life" are application oriented.) At least one-third of the small group discussion time should be spent discussing application of the truth. It is often tempting to get caught up in the content part of the study, but you, as the leader, are responsible to move the group along to application.

A word needs to be said about the relationship between Pocket Principles® and Guided Discussions. The content of both is generally the same, although not identical. These 2 formats provide different ways of presenting the same content, or both can be used to reinforce the content. (Another type of WDA material is Teaching Outlines. These are designed to be used by a teacher who wants to present the content in a lecture format to a larger group. Free Teaching Outlines can be downloaded from www.disciplebuilding.org/materials/growing-spiritually-teaching-outlines-free-download.

There are two (2) versions of each study: the Leader's version with answers and special notes, and the Student version with questions, but no answers. *Answers and notes to leaders are in gray, italicized text.*

Much of the preparation has been done for you as a leader: topics have been chosen, Scriptures chosen, questions written. However, it is important that you become comfortable with the material so that you will be able to be flexible and focus on the needs of your group. In the *Small Groups Manual* (WDA), you will find information about the practical aspects of group leadership. Please refer to the section titled "Practical Dynamics of Small Group Leadership." This is available from the WDA store at www.disciplebuilding.org/store/leadership-manuals/small-groups-manual.

God's Plan For The Believer

Some years back, after Henry Norris Russell, the Princeton astronomer, had concluded a lecture on the Milky Way, a woman came to him and asked, "If our world is so little, and the universe is so great, can we believe God really pays any attention to us?" Dr. Russell replied, "That depends, madam, entirely on how big a God you believe in."

ONE OF OUR GREATEST NEEDS IS TO HAVE A PURPOSE IN LIFE.

God has built into each one of us a desire to do something meaningful with our lives—to make a contribution. The American naturalist and author Henry David Thoreau wrote toward the end of a life in which he could find no ultimate meaning that "most of us live lives of quiet desperation." While his statement is perhaps overly pessimistic, it is generally agreed that most people seem to be seeking for something more out of life than they are able to find. The good news is that not only does God instill that desire within us, but He also has a plan for each of us to satisfy that desire and to find great meaning and significance in our lives. Along with the astronomer Russell, we worship a God big enough to create the universe and gracious enough to design a special place for us in it.

GOD HAS A PLAN FOR EACH BELIEVER.

God grants both the need for meaning and the opportunity to find it. This has been part of His master plan from the beginning. As Paul wrote to the believers at Ephesus, "We are God's masterpiece. He has created us anew in Christ Jesus, so that we can do the good things He planned for us long ago." (Ephesians 2:10, *New Living Translation*) In the original language of Scripture, the word "masterpiece" literally means "poem." Think of your life as a poem written by God, with each day a new opportunity to do the things that He has planned for you to do. As living poems, we find meaning and significance in fulfilling the desire of the Author of the universe.

...we worship a God big enough to create the universe and gracious enough to design a special place for us in it.

God's design involves both privilege and responsibility. Philippians chapter two, verses 12 and 13 say, "Dearest friends, you were always so careful to follow my instructions when I was with you. And now that I am away you must be even more careful to put into action God's saving work in your lives, obeying God with deep reverence and fear. For God is working in you, giving you the desire to obey Him and the power to do what pleases Him." (*New Living Translation*) Note that the verbs are active on both sides of the equation. The believer's role is by no means passive. As Paul reminds the Christians in Philippi, we have a responsibility to do the things that please God. However, he also reminds them that it is God who gives the ability to fulfill the responsibility.

GOD PROGRESSIVELY REVEALS HIS PLAN FOR EACH BELIEVER.

Once we understand that God has things for us to do, we must think through how we come to understand what it is that He expects us to do. The believer is not given a playbook at the time of salvation or upon being baptized or joining a church. In reality, the rest of the believer's life is a process of discovering and doing the will of God. In His infinite wisdom, God reveals His plan more fully as we grow in spiritual maturity and understanding. This is similar to the work of an artist who starts first with the background and covers the canvas with broad strokes. Then he paints in the major points of interest. Finally, he fills in the details.

God's plan for the believer has both an internal component (spiritual growth) and an external component (ministry). The internal is "being" and the external is "doing." The internal component has priority. We must *be* what God wants us to be before we can *do* what God wants us to do. Ministry (the external component) is an overflow of the inner life. However, ministry is also a means of future growth. So we see a circle where spiritual growth leads to ministry, and ministry leads to more spiritual growth.

The general expectations that God has of all who follow Him are woven throughout Scripture, in both the Old Testament and the New. These expectations generally focus on the believer's inner life and include such things as maintaining an attitude of prayer and dependence on God, keeping ourselves pure, giving thanks in all situations, being kind and considerate to others, and so on.

Specific expectations, or details of the plan, often revolve around the good works (ministry) that God has planned for us to do. One of the primary ways that we fulfill our purpose is by using our spiritual gifts. Scripture makes it clear that God's Holy Spirit has endowed each believer with one or more spiritual gifts in keeping with His master plan. As we develop and use these gifts to His glory, we are fulfilling our role in His plan. Other dynamics are at work that help define God's will in our lives (personality, interests, passions, etc.), but these will be discussed in other publications.

When it comes to discovering God's will for their lives, many Christians seem most concerned with major decisions such as who to marry, what career to pursue, where to live, and so on. We don't find this preoccupation in Scripture.

Rather, the emphasis there is on godliness and ministry. These twin pursuits provide a context in which to make the other decisions.

At each point along this path, God presents us with ministry opportunities that are appropriate for our level of spiritual maturity. Consider the example of a father who wants to teach his son carpentry. The father, himself a master craftsman, can see from the beginning the potential of his apprentice and the beautiful objects he will someday create. However, he starts with very simple tasks. In the early years, the son's primary responsibility is to watch his father and to help when asked. The father starts by teaching his son how to use simple tools. He gives him scrap pieces of wood to practice on. As the son gains physical strength and maturity, the father increases the level of responsibility. At some point, he allows the son to begin using power tools. Once the son gains proficiency, the father gives him the opportunity to work on real projects, but always under the father's close instruction and watchful eye. After many years of instruction and development, the son is ready to use any tool to tackle any project.

So it is with our heavenly Father as He develops His workmanship into workers. Just as a wise and considerate father would never give a young boy a dangerous power tool and leave him alone to complete a complex project, so our Father does not require of us anything beyond our capability. We see this pattern in the life of Christ as He worked with His disciples. From a relational perspective, Jesus asked His followers first only to trust in Him as the Messiah they had been looking for, then as their provider and protector, and finally as One who desired and was able to work through them. From a ministry perspective, Jesus first took His disciples with Him so they could observe. Gradually, He began to give them more responsibility and involve them in the ministry. Finally, He sent them out on their own.

> We must be what God wants us to be before we can do what God wants us to do.

Over a period of many months together, the conversations between Jesus and His disciples went from "Come and see" to "Follow me" to "Work with me" to the point where He could finally tell His disciples on the night before His crucifixion, "As the Father has sent me, so I am sending you." And also, "You shall do greater works than you have seen me do." It would have been absurd for Jesus to utter the last statements as soon as His disciples began to follow Him, but from the beginning His design was to prepare them to hear and respond to these words.

GOD WORKS OUT HIS PLAN IN THE MIDST OF THE CHALLENGES OF LIFE.

If God's only desire were to bring us safely home to glory, He could easily choose to arrange things so that Christians would be protected and immune from all the bad things of life. But because He desires for us to grow into His likeness, to be His agents for change in this world and to help accomplish His purposes, He allows us to face life as it comes and teaches us in and through these circumstances.

Challenges are a daily fact of life for the child of God. These difficulties come from any number of sources including our own sin nature, the fallen world, the sins of others, spiritual warfare, human limitations, emotional issues, and sometimes even from God Himself. Because of these challenges, the working out of God's plan is not a smooth process. It is often not predictable, easy, or comfortable. In fact, the path we are called to follow is often difficult, sometimes painful, confusing, and dangerous, and may even appear to be a dead end at times.

There is much written in Scripture about the role trials and troubles play in the Christian's life. James, the brother of Jesus, wrote that we are to joyfully welcome difficulties as friends because of the good that they accomplish in our lives. Granted, this can be a difficult thing to do in the midst of the trial. But we should focus on the outcome, knowing that challenges, when responded to properly, produce perseverance, endurance, strength of character, and spiritual maturity. In short, they help conform us to the image of Christ. An important point to remember is that there is nothing that comes into our lives that cannot be redeemed by God for our good and for His glory.

To further understand the role of difficulties, let's return to the earlier illustration of a painting. The artist starts first with the background and covers the canvas in broad strokes. Then he begins to add the details. A frequently used technique to add definition and focus to a painting is to use darker colors for contrast, adding outline, shadow, and depth. So it is with the difficult challenges—the darker colors—that God uses to bring greater clarity to His plans for us. Challenges are part of the plan. Difficulties give definition to the picture, and make it come more clearly into focus.

GOD LINKS HIS PLAN FOR EACH BELIEVER WITH HIS GREATER PLAN FOR ALL CREATION.

Dallas Willard writes in *The Divine Conspiracy*, "It is always true that meaning is found, when it is found, in some larger context." A further element of significance for believers is that we play a role in the larger scheme of things. It is

God's design to involve us in His unfolding drama of redemption. Ours are not simply unrelated bit parts to fill time between scenes. Rather we are players on the stage of human history with significant roles to play.

Throughout history, God has chosen to use humans to accomplish His purposes. We see this consistently throughout Scripture. Then it was an Abraham, a Moses, a Ruth, a David, or a Mary. Today it may be a Fred or a Tiffany or a Charles. Reading through the written record, we can plainly see how God had determined for people to be involved in His plan. It is often not as easy to see or even to believe that we also are part of His plan. But this is the startling truth.

> Throughout history, God has chosen to use humans to accomplish His purposes.

When John the Baptizer came to prepare the way for the Messiah, he proclaimed, "Repent, for the Kingdom of God is at hand." As Jesus walked and ministered among the people, he taught, "The kingdom of heaven is among you." And so the kingdom of God has already been established in the hearts and lives of those who have chosen to follow Jesus. And it continues to grow today as His Word goes out and more are brought to faith in Christ. As we fulfill His plan for our lives, we are doing kingdom work. And Scripture tells us that someday we will rule with Christ when He establishes His eternal reign. Significant work indeed!

SUMMARY

The things that we have considered should bring great joy to the heart of every believer. Each of us can have full confidence that our lives have purpose and meaning because of the following truths:

1. God has a plan for every believer, which He progressively reveals to us.

2. God works out His plan through and in the difficult challenges of life.

3. We are part of God's larger plan for the whole world.

God's Plan For The Believer

IMPORTANT to Leader: Answers and notes to leaders are in gray, italicized text.

GOAL:

For a disciple to understand that God has a plan for each believer that is a part of His overall plan for His kingdom.

GETTING STARTED:

Picture this:

You work on the assembly line for a carmaker. Your assembly line installs the brake system. Your specific task is to attach the brake pedal to the master cylinder (i.e. the brake system). What would happen if everyone on the line did his job, except you?

Transition: Just as it is important that each person on an assembly line fulfills his task, it is also important for each believer to carry out the task/role he has been given by God, which is part of His overall plan for His kingdom.

STUDYING TOGETHER:

Read Ephesians 1:9-10.

1. According to Ephesians 1:9, what privilege has God given New Testament believers?

    He has revealed the mystery to us.

2. According to Ephesians 1:10, what is God's plan (the "mystery") for the world?

    To bring all things in heaven and on earth together under one Head, Christ.

    When will this plan culminate?

    When the times have reached their fulfillment (when Christ returns).

Read Ephesians 2:10.

3. According to Ephesians 2:10, what is our involvement in God's plan?

    To take part in that plan by doing good works that God has prepared for each of us.

What two things does God do, and what is the relationship between the two?

  1) *He has prepared in advance the good works we are to do and He builds us ("we are His workmanship").*
  2) *God builds us up so that we can carry out the good works He has prepared.*

4. Ephesians 1:9-10 is about God's overall plan, and Ephesians 2:10 is about God's plan for the individual believer. What is the relationship between the two?

    The plan for the individual is a part of the plan for the whole world.

Read James 1:2-5.

5. How does God use challenges and difficulties in this process of individual growth?

    He uses difficulties to develop faith and perseverance which culminates in spiritual maturity.

6. To this point in your Christian life, how has God revealed Himself and His will to you: slowly and progressively or quickly and completely? Explain.

    God usually uses both in our lives, but in neither case does He show the believer all of His will at one time.

Jesus' ministry to the Twelve is the best example of progressive revelation of His will. For example, regarding trusting Him: Jesus first asked them to trust that He was the Messiah (John 1:35-42). Later He wanted them to trust Him for provision and protection (John 6:1-12) and eventually to work through them (Luke 9:1-2).

LOOKING AT REAL LIFE:

7. What is the main reason that some Christians believe that God will not work through them?

    Past failure, a feeling of insecurity, lack of faith in God, etc.

8. Why do you think God doesn't give us the details of His overall plan right now?

LOOKING AT MY LIFE:

Describe an event in your life that didn't make sense at the time, but today, makes sense as it pertains to God's overall plan.

What is happening in your life right now that doesn't make any sense to you regarding how it fits into God's overall plan? Pray for one another in groups of 3 or 4, asking God to give you the strength, wisdom, and faith needed to keep trusting God.

Knowing God's Will

One of the most common questions believers ask is, "How can I know God's will?" This is a healthy question and reflects a desire to understand and to do the things that please God. Understanding God's will is also necessary for spiritual growth. Unfortunately, in modern society where instant answers and clear solutions have become expected, some Christians can get frustrated when they find it difficult to know God's will, or it is not as clear as they would like it to be. Whether it is how to lose 30 pounds in three months, how to become financially secure, or how to overcome a bad habit or addiction, we have become accustomed to having someone provide us with a certain number of steps to follow that are guaranteed to achieve the desired outcome.

It is important to remember that God is not our enemy. We are not playing some game of hide and seek where we are desperately seeking to find something that God is enjoying hiding from us. Christ's words to His disciples the night before His crucifixion should be an encouragement to us. He reminded them that they had entered a new relationship with Him, and He had now taken them into His confidence and revealed the Father's will to them. We enjoy the same close relationship with our Lord and can rest assured that He also desires to make the Father's business known to us.

While there are no easy answers and no set formulas to follow, we can understand the will of God by humbly responding to the truth He reveals. Following are some of the most common ways God reveals His will.

THE BIBLE

In his second letter to Timothy, the Apostle Paul reminded him that the holy Scriptures are given by God to make us wise and to help us discern what we should do. II Timothy 3:16-17 says, "All Scripture is God-breathed and is useful for teaching, rebuking, correcting and training in righteousness, so that the servant of God may be thoroughly equipped for every good work." Or, as the *New Living Translation* puts it, "It is God's way of preparing us in every way, fully equipped for every good thing God wants us to do." Not only does Scripture reveal the character of God and how we can grow in godliness, but it also prepares us for the specific things that He wants us to do.

The Apostle Peter told his readers that they should desire the pure spiritual milk of the Word as a newborn baby desires her mother's milk. It is the primary means of growth for the believer. Regular, daily feeding will ensure that our thinking is informed by the Word. Not only is understanding the will of God necessary for spiritual growth, but spiritual growth is important in understanding the will of God. As the believer matures in her Christian walk, she gains more insight into the Word of God and is better able to understand and to apply the principles found in it.

Broadly speaking, when attempting to discern the will of God, the believer should look in Scripture for general principles to apply rather than expecting to find specific guidance. Humorous stories are told of individuals who have opened the Bible, put their fingers on the page, and then made decisions based on whatever they happened to read first. One such man, who was deeply in debt, found that his finger landed on Chapter 11 and went out and filed bankruptcy. As unlikely as this story may be, it does remind us of the danger of using Scripture inappropriately.

PRAYER

Prayer is one of the primary means by which we can determine God's leading. James 1:5 says that if anyone lacks wisdom (the ability to determine the right course of action), he should ask God, and God will freely and gladly respond to this request. Jesus, after teaching His disciples to pray, reminded them of the need for perseverance. He then promised that "everyone who asks receives; the one who seeks finds; and to the one who knocks, the door will be opened." (Luke 11:10)

> We can understand the will of God by humbly responding to the truth He reveals.

The Bible is full of examples of saints of the past who inquired of God when facing a decision and received the wisdom needed to take the right course of action (see, for example, the victories of King David recorded in II Samuel 5:17-25). Scripture also records the disastrous consequences when people jumped into action without waiting on God for direction (see, for example, the defeat of King Josiah recorded in II Chronicles 35:20-24).

PROMPTING OF THE HOLY SPIRIT

The Holy Spirit plays many roles in the life of the believer, and one of the primary ones is to provide guidance. Jesus referred to the Spirit as the Counselor and indicated that He would teach and direct us. The Holy Spirit is a trusted counselor who confirms truth within our hearts by giving us peace and confidence to move forward. He will withhold this sense of peace if we are heading in the wrong direction.

Another primary function of the Spirit is to point out the sin in our lives. Sin clouds our vision and distorts our view of things, making it impossible for us to see God's leading. Worse yet, sin can cause us to be unable even to realize that our vision is faulty. When we allow Him the freedom to operate in our lives, the Holy Spirit acts with surgical precision to remove the sinful cataracts from our eyes and renew our vision.

Some Christians are uncomfortable trusting the Spirit for guidance because they fear it allows too much subjectivity into the process. However, the role of the Spirit is to confirm within our hearts the objective truth of the Word of God. George Mueller, who cared for thousands of orphans in 19th century England and was known as a man of great faith and prayer explains, "I will seek the will of the Spirit of God through, or in connection with, the Word of God. The Spirit and the Word must be combined. If I look to the Spirit alone without the Word, I lay myself open to great delusions also. If the Holy Spirit guides us at all, He will do it according to the Scriptures and never contrary to them." (From Mueller's sermon "Pilgrim and Sojourner")

THE PEOPLE OF GOD

Fellow believers are another resource we can draw on to understand the will of God. Proverbs 20:18 reminds us to make plans by seeking advice. It is part of God's design for the church that more mature believers and those gifted at teaching are to teach the Word to younger believers (I Timothy 3:11-14). This mentoring approach includes communicating not only principles found in Scripture, but also the appropriate application of those principles in everyday life.

An example of the biblical pattern is found in Acts chapter 15. Differences of opinion had arisen in the early church regarding the extent to which Gentile believers should be required to keep the Jewish law. Leaders in the church met together in Jerusalem to seek God's will concerning this situation. Acts 15:6 records that the apostles and elders met to consider this question. It was only after much open discussion that Peter stood up to address the assembly. Then further exchanges took place before the group finally reached a consensus decision regarding the direction they should take.

CIRCUMSTANCES

God expects the believer to use her mind in the process of discovering His will. One of the ways that we meet this expectation is to make sense of the world around us—the circumstances that come our way. Often, a common sense approach toward interpreting political, social, economic, or other events will guide us to the right plan of action. For example, a person may be considering adding an addition to his house, one that would take it to within fourteen feet of a right of way. If the local authorities pass an ordinance restricting construction within 25 feet of a right of way, then the person no longer needs to consider whether it is God's will for him to build the addition.

We should also consider the circumstances of our existence. God has created each of us as a unique human being, with a complex blend of abilities, interests, and desires. Surely these factors—God's design—should be taken into account when determining His will for us. It is highly unlikely that God's will for a short, slow young man with no interest in sports is for him to play professional basketball. However, a young lady who is extremely talented musically and has a strong desire to perform may well be led of God to use those abilities and to satisfy that desire by performing to His glory.

CONCLUSION

Although there is not a set formula for knowing God's will, God often reveals His will in the ways we have considered. Equally important, if not more so, than the means of discovering God's will is the mindset we have while searching for direction. God will bless us as we exhibit the following attitudes.

Submission. "Whatever it turns out to be, I'll do it." Some Christians wrongly believe that they can ask God for direction and then decide whether or not they want to obey the marching orders they receive. Others simply look for confirmation of what they've already decided they want to do. Either approach betrays a stubborn resistance to the Lordship of Christ in our lives. The fact is that God reveals more of Himself and His will to us as we walk in obedience. Remember that it is in the context of obedience that Jesus spoke of His new relationship with His disciples and the revelation of the Father's will to them (John 15).

Humility. "I know I don't have all the answers." The story is told of an old sailor who repeatedly got lost at sea, so his friends gave him a compass and urged him to use it. The next time he went out in his boat, he followed their advice and took the compass with him. But as usual he became hopelessly confused and was unable to find land. Finally, he was rescued by his friends. Disgusted and impatient with him, they asked, "Why didn't you use that compass we gave you? You could have saved us a lot of trouble!" The sailor responded, "I didn't dare to! I wanted to go north, but as hard as I tried to make the needle aim in that direction, it just kept on pointing southeast." Our pride tells us that we know best or that we don't need anyone to tell us what to do. We must strive for a posture of humility that expresses itself in a teachable spirit and a willingness to learn from others.

> God reveals more of Himself and His will to us as we walk in obedience.

Patience. "I'm willing to wait as long as it takes." Determining God's will is often not easy. It may involve waiting on God and wrestling with Him about the decision. Noted theologian and author James Packer reminds us, " 'Wait on the Lord' is a constant refrain in the Psalms and it is a necessary word, for the

Lord often keeps us waiting. When in doubt, do nothing, but continue to wait on God." We can rest assured that God will never keep us waiting longer than is necessary to accomplish His purposes. However, He knows that the process may be as important as the outcome.

Psalm 119:105 speaks of God's Word as a lamp to our feet and a light to our path. It is not referred to as a floodlight to illumine the road ahead. Often we have only enough light to take the next step on the path, but that is sufficient if we are willing to trust the One leading us. In this process of seeking God's will, we would do well to remember the prayer of Richard of Chichester, a saint of the early 13th century: "Day by day, dear Lord, of Thee, three things I pray. To see Thee more clearly, to love Thee more dearly, to follow Thee more nearly, day by day."

Knowing God's Will

GOAL:

For a disciple to understand how to know God's will for her life and to recognize general aspects of God's will.

GETTING STARTED:

If you got lost driving in an unfamiliar area, which of the following would be your first instinct? Explain why.

☐ keep driving around until you find your destination

☐ stop and ask for directions at a gas station

☐ look at a map

☐ call someone for directions

☐ pray

Transition: All of us are on the road to somewhere. In today's lesson, we will learn about the path that God has laid out for every believer.

STUDYING TOGETHER:

Read Ephesians 2:10.

1. According to Ephesians 2:10, how are believers described?

   God's workmanship.

   What does this verse indicate about our lives?

   God has an individual plan for every believer's life. Generally, God reveals His plan to a believer a little at a time as the believer grows spiritually.

14

2. Using the following verses, identify the various ways that God reveals His will to believers.

   a. Psalm 119:105; II Timothy 3:16-17

      The Bible teaches about God's will as well as His character.

   b. James 1:5

      Through prayer we can ascertain God's will.

   c. Acts 16:6-10

      The prompting of the Holy Spirit is an inner sense of confirmation of truth and/or a conviction of sin. God also may speak to His people through visions.

   d. Ephesians 4:11-13; Acts 15:2,6

      More mature believers and those gifted at teaching are to teach the Word to younger believers; insight into the will of God can be gained through interaction with other believers.

   e. Acts 8:1,4

      God may use circumstances to direct/redirect us to His will. Here, God used the persecution to force His people to preach the Word elsewhere.

3. Using the following verses, identify some behaviors that God's Word clearly states as being His will:

   a. I Thessalonians 4:3

      God wants us to grow spiritually; He wants us to be sexually pure.

   b. I Thessalonians 5:18

      God wants us to be thankful in all circumstances.

   c. Romans 13:1

      God wants us to submit to the governing authorities.

d. I Peter 4:10

God wants us to serve others.

e. II Corinthians 6:14-15

Applying these verses to marriage, they indicate that God's will is for a Christian to be yoked together in marriage to another Christian.

4. After examining the Scriptures in question # 3 above, how helpful is the Bible in helping us know God's will?

Much of God's will is clearly stated in His word.

LOOKING AT REAL LIFE:

5. How do you think most Christians approach the issue of knowing God's will?

☐ It's like looking for a needle in a haystack…I'll never know it.

☐ It can't really be known for sure…just go with your gut feeling.

☐ We can only do the best we can now…God will sort it all out in the end.

☐ God's Word is the best place to start and reveals much of God's will already.

☐ other: _____

6. Why do you think there is so much frustration among believers concerning the issue of God's will?

LOOKING AT MY LIFE:

In the following areas, what do you already know about God's will for your life right now? Spend a few minutes and write down one sentence beside each area describing what you are sure of. Also, write one sentence about what you are unsure of in each area.

Job/employment—

Marriage/family—

Finances—

Serving others—

In groups of 2 or 3, share the area concerning God's will that you are struggling with the most. Pray for one another concerning these struggles, asking God for wisdom.

The Process Of Spiritual Growth

The story is told of a group of tourists who were touring a village. An old man was seated on a park bench, and one of the tourists asked him if any great men had been born in the small town. "No," the man replied after a moment's thought, "only babies."

Just as no man or woman is born great, no Christian is mature immediately upon being born into the family of God. Each believer starts this new life as a babe in Christ. However, it is God's plan for every believer to grow from spiritual infancy to spiritual maturity. He gives us the resources we need and provides a model for us to follow. We can understand the process of spiritual growth by examining principles seen in the life of Jesus.

THE GOAL OF SPIRITUAL GROWTH IS CHRIST-LIKE CHARACTER.

It is natural for the new believer to ask: "What does spiritual maturity look like?" The answer is that it looks like Jesus Christ. He not only is the object of our faith, but He is the object of our growth. From the beginning, God's desire has been for those who believe in Christ to be conformed to His likeness (Romans 8:29). As we grow in Christ and become more like Him, those around us should be able to see His image reflected in us (II Corinthians 3:18). This does not mean that we will become physically like Him, with the same appearance, mannerisms, or manner of speaking. Rather, it means that we will become like Him in our attitudes and in our actions.

The Christian life is all about relationships.

This is a lofty goal indeed and can be intimidating, especially to the new believer. However, it is important to remember that God provides us with more than the minimum daily requirements for our spiritual growth. In fact, II Peter 1:3 says that God's divine power has given us everything we need for life and godliness. Some Christians find this hard to believe, especially when they begin to experience challenges or frustration in their spiritual lives. And, sadly, there are sometimes people who mistakenly tell them that they don't have everything they need—that to really grow they need something more. This "something more" may be a mystical experience, a special anointing from the Holy Spirit, a special degree of wisdom or knowledge, or something else. Regardless of how well-intended this advice may be, it is a form of spiritual intimidation and should be rejected as such. Just as a healthy baby is born with all the parts it needs to grow and develop normally, so do we Christians begin our new lives in Christ.

18

SPIRITUAL GROWTH OCCURS GRADUALLY, IN PHASES.

One error to avoid is thinking that God has not given us everything we need to grow. An equally dangerous wrong belief is that growth will occur overnight. Just as a newborn baby develops gradually and only after much nourishment and the proper care, so it is with the babe in Christ. We should expect to drink milk before we can eat meat, and to crawl before we can walk. God understands this better than we do, and He patiently works with us as He conforms us to the image of His Son. We see this principle illustrated in the approach Christ took with His disciples.

A careful study of the life and ministry of Christ will show that He was deliberate in the way that He related to and worked with His disciples. Because each of the Gospel writers recorded the life of Christ from his own perspective, it can be difficult to see a pattern simply by reading through the New Testament. However, when the Gospel accounts are combined into a chronological narrative, it is clear that Jesus taught His disciples things that were appropriate for each phase of growth, and that He moved them through successive phases. It is also clear that Jesus intended this pattern to be repeated as, before His return to heaven, He commanded His followers to make disciples in all nations, teaching the same things He had taught.

While people may label these phases differently, they can be described as follows:

1) *Coming to faith* — The necessary first step for anyone to become a disciple of Christ is to repent of his sins and former way of life and to trust in Christ as his Savior. This event is referred to in Scripture as being born again (John 3). Regardless of whether a person comes to faith at age eight or eighty-eight, he becomes a newborn babe in Christ.

2) *Laying foundations* — The focus of this early phase in the life of the believer is gaining a better understanding of who Christ is and how to follow Him. As the new Christian learns more of Christ's nature and character, she learns to trust Him not only for salvation but for other things as well. During this phase, Jesus invited His disciples to spend more time with Him so that He could reveal Himself more fully to them.

3) *Ministry involvement and training* — In this phase, the disciple learns to serve others and engages in ministry opportunities under the guidance of more mature believers. Jesus' call to His disciples, "Follow me and I will make you fishers of men," indicates that He was moving them to the next phase of growth. Jesus took His disciples with Him as He went about teaching and ministering to people.

4) *Leadership*—As the believer progresses to this phase, he is ready to take responsibility for the spiritual well being of others. Jesus' time during this phase with His disciples was characterized by teaching about how to live in His Kingdom. Also, He designated twelve of His closest disciples as apostles and sent them out on their own to preach the Kingdom of God and to minister to people's needs.

THERE ARE TWO DIMENSIONS TO SPIRITUAL GROWTH— EQUIPPING AND RESTORING.

Not only does spiritual growth occur in phases, but it also involves two dimensions—equipping and restoring. The equipping dimension includes building knowledge, skills, and abilities into peoples' lives, while the restoring dimension refers to regaining the image of God by developing emotional and relational health. The phases discussed above relate primarily to the equipping dimension, which is characterized by growth in such areas as personal knowledge of Christ and His ways, the ability to trust God, and the ability to minister to others.

The second dimension relates to our emotional and relational well-being. This aspect is necessary because, when a person comes to faith in Christ, she brings all of her baggage along with her. Some of us bring little baggage and some of us bring a lot, but none of us has the emotional and relational health necessary to grow to full maturity in Christ. As can be seen in the way Christ worked with His disciples, God does not wait to complete the equipping dimension before He begins to work on the restoring dimension. Rather, the two are interrelated and He works on them at the same time. In fact, it must be so because one can only grow so far spiritually if emotional or relational issues are not addressed.

> There is no relational health without emotional health.

Because of our own sin nature and because we live in a fallen world, we develop unhealthy patterns of thinking and behaving as we make our way through life. Many of these patterns develop as we try to protect ourselves from the inevitable hurts that come our way. God wants to restore us to emotional health, not just so we can minister effectively for Him, but primarily so that we can enjoy our relationship with Him and with others. There is no relational health without emotional health.

As in all other areas, Jesus is our model of emotional and relational well-being. It is an understatement to say that not everyone liked Him, but the way He related to friends and foes alike was healthy. His words and actions were characterized by integrity, purity, and honesty. And His emotions betrayed integrity as well. As G. Walter Hansenin writes in *Christianity Today*, "I am spellbound by the intensity of Jesus' emotions: Not a twinge of pity, but heartbroken compassion; not a passing irritation, but terrifying anger; not a silent tear, but groans of anguish; not a weak smile, but ecstatic celebration. Jesus' emotions are like a mountain river cascading with clear water. My emotions are more like a muddy foam or a feeble trickle."[1] Because of the hurts in our past and the resulting protective behaviors we have engaged in, many of us can probably identify more closely with the description of Mr. Hansenin's emotions than we can with those of Jesus.

The Christian life is all about relationships. When we place our faith in Christ, we enter into relationship with Him. We also become part of the family of God. The Bible speaks of believers as members of the Body of Christ. Much of the teaching of the New Testament revolves around how we are to relate to one another. If we have not developed emotional and relational health, these new relationships can be very challenging. The good news is that these new relationships provide a wonderful opportunity for us to grow. Believers should make up a restoring community, where we demonstrate unconditional acceptance and speak the truth to one another in love (Ephesians 4:15).

CONCLUSION

In light of these teachings, our primary concern should be that we see consistent progress over time in our spiritual growth and that this growth is evident in all areas of our lives. We should imitate the Apostle Paul's mindset as reflected when he wrote, "...I press on to take hold of that for which Christ Jesus took hold of me. Brothers, I do not consider myself yet to have taken hold of it. But one thing I do: Forgetting what is behind and straining toward what is ahead, I press on toward the goal to win the prize for which God has called me heavenward in Christ Jesus." (Philippians 3:12-14). The picture Paul paints is of an athlete who is straining every muscle as he pushes toward the goal. We should exhibit the same determination in our spiritual lives.

However, we should not become preoccupied with growth for growth's sake. We should not become like the anxious six-year-old boy who every morning jumps out of bed and runs over to the growth chart taped to the back of his door to see if he has grown any taller over night. If we continue to press toward the mark, growth will come. And, each day we can rejoice in the confidence that He who has begun this good work in us will carry it through to completion (Philippians 1:6).

End Note:

(1) G. Walter Hansenin, "An Awesome God," *Christianity Today*, February 6, 2008.

The Process Of Spiritual Growth

IMPORTANT to Leader: Answers and notes to leaders are in gray, italicized text.

GOALS:

For a disciple to understand the meaning of growing in Christlikeness.

For a disciple to evaluate where he is in his spiritual development.

GETTING STARTED:

Children grow and develop in many areas. What are some of these areas?

Physical, social, academic, etc.

Transition: We are able to recognize physical growth (as well as other areas of growth) in children by the skills they are developing. In a similar way, we can recognize spiritual growth in our lives by the characteristics we begin to exhibit.

STUDYING TOGETHER:

Read II Peter 1:5-8.

1. What does this passage teach about spiritual growth?

    There are several correct answers to this question, e.g. character is necessary, growth requires effort on the believer's part, etc. The answer we want to focus on is that spiritual growth is PROGRESSIVE, that is, a predictable, sequential process (II Corinthians 3:18; James 1:2-4).

2. What do you think the goal of spiritual growth is?

    Allow group participants to respond.

Read II Corinthians 3:18 and Romans 8:29.

3. According to these two verses, what is the goal of spiritual growth?

    Christlikeness

4. What characteristic of Christlikeness is found in each of the following verses?

Colossians 1:9-10

Growing in the knowledge of God and His will & obeying Him

How does a person grow in the knowledge of God?

Read the Bible, pray, listen to good teaching, have fellowship.

How does a person grow in obedience?

Trust God the Holy Spirit to fill and empower, have an accountability partner, have a specific plan, deal with root emotional issues.

I Peter 1:15-16

Growing in holiness

What is holiness?

To be set apart; moral perfection, moral purity

Describe what holiness looks like in a person's life.

He exhibits love, integrity, right priorities, sexual purity, faithfulness, all the fruit of the Spirit.

I John 3:16-18, 4:7

Growing in love

How do you show love to others?

Read James 1:2-4 and Romans 8:28.

5. According to these verses, what role do difficulties play in spiritual growth?

   Encourage it, challenge a believer to grow, give new areas to trust God in, helps us see our need for God.

Read Matthew 28:18-20.

6. In verse 20, what does Jesus tell His disciples to do after He leaves them?

    Teach people to obey everything Christ taught them.

7. We in WDA have studied "everything" Jesus taught them, and have discovered that Jesus guided His disciples through specific patterns of spiritual growth, or Phases. These are:

    Phase I: Coming to Faith Phase

    Phase II: Laying Foundations Phase (learn who Christ is and how to follow Him) (The lessons in this series are focused on the Laying Foundations Phase.)

    Phase III: Ministry Training Phase

    Phases IV and V: Leadership Phases

LOOKING AT REAL LIFE:

8. What difficulties have you seen in believers' lives that have helped them grow spiritually?

9. Who has helped you most in your spiritual growth? What did (or does) this person do to help you grow?

LOOKING AT MY LIFE:

Evaluate your progress in growing into Christlikeness by using the scales to describe your progress. Use the following as a scale: 1-2 = Desiring to grow; 3-4 = Just beginning; 5-6 = Getting going, moving along. Then, write a sentence explaining your response.

Growing in the knowledge of God and His will.

1   2   3   4   5   6

Growing in holiness.

1   2   3   4   5   6

Growing in helping others.

1   2   3   4   5   6

Divide into pairs and discuss the following questions:

Which of the three areas in the "Looking at My Life" section did you rate the weakest and why?

What is one practical step you can take this week to make progress in that area?

How can others pray for you concerning your progress as you grow in Christlikeness?

Close your time by praying in pairs concerning the one practical step you have shared.

Dimensions Of Spiritual Growth

Scientists marvel at the inter-connected nature of all living organisms. Though many stubbornly refuse to recognize the fingerprints of God in creation, they still speak in awe of the complex design of things they observe and refer to the delicate balance of nature. Because we are complex beings, understanding spiritual growth demands that we understand many components of our lives. To attain spiritual maturity the believer must grow in at least two dimensions of the Christian life—equipping and restoring. The equipping dimension prepares the believer to serve others on behalf of Jesus, in effect, to carry on His work, while the restoring dimension addresses a person's emotional and relational health.

Historically, the church has focused primarily on the equipping dimension of the believer's life and has not always recognized the need to minister to the whole person. This limited perspective of the church's calling is a tragic misunderstanding that has hindered not only the growth of individual believers but also the ability of the church to impact the world for Christ. *From our experience,* we have concluded that healthy spiritual growth is most likely to occur when both dimensions (equipping and restoring) are addressed.

THE EQUIPPING DIMENSION INVOLVES GROWING IN THE FOLLOWING AREAS:

Growth in knowledge of God, His ways, and His will

Knowledge of God, including His character, His ways, and His will is essential to spiritual growth. The Apostle Paul's understanding of this principle led him to pray for the believers in Colossae as follows: "We have not stopped praying for you and asking God to fill you with the knowledge of His will through all spiritual wisdom and understanding. And we pray this in order that you might live a life worthy of the Lord and may please Him in every way: bearing fruit in every good work, growing in the knowledge of God." (Colossians 1:9-10)

Paul's prayer for these believers provides insight into the dynamics of spiritual growth. The more we grow in spiritual wisdom, the more we will live lives pleasing to God, doing the good things He desires us to do. This action leads to a greater knowledge of God and more spiritual wisdom. And so the circle of growth continues.

The knowledge of God that Paul writes about is interactive and experiential, not just an accumulation of information. An example will help make this point. A person can study the sport of scuba diving, can watch others scuba dive, and can even speak intelligently about scuba diving, but until she actually puts on the equipment and dives into the water, she is not a scuba diver. Similarly, many people who know much about what the Bible teaches have not embraced the teachings of Scripture as truth in their hearts and put it into action. They may know about God, but they do not know God.

In addition, to grow spiritually, a believer needs to interact with other believers in a local church body. Paul in I Corinthians 12 makes it clear that believers, as members of the Body of Christ, are inter-dependent on each other. They are to express this inter-dependence by showing love for each other, learning from each other and praying for one another. This interaction with other believers can significantly impact the spiritual growth as the young believer is encouraged and provided with real-life models of the Christian life.

Another area that influences spiritual growth is the specific content of a believer's learning. The early focus of learning needs to be centered on such subjects as God's character, who Jesus is, and how to walk with Jesus daily. These topics are necessary for a healthy relationship with God and a strong foundation for further growth. As we grasp a basic knowledge of who God is, we learn how to please Him, and follow His leading. We gain this knowledge through daily interaction with God in the circumstances of life.

Growth in ministry skills and abilities (Mark 10:45)

As mentioned above, the point of acquiring knowledge is so that it can be put into action. One of the ways we act on our knowledge of God is to minister to others or, as Paul puts it, "bearing fruit in every good work." (Colossians 1:10) In the early phases of the Christian's walk, his focus needs to be meeting the practical needs of others (e.g. arranging transportation, cooking meals, etc.). We see this principle in the way Jesus taught His followers how to minister. When His disciples were new believers, Jesus gave them practical responsibilities such as dispensing food, providing transportation, controlling the crowds, and bringing their friends to learn about Him.

As believers grow spiritually, God often increases their ministry abilities and opportunities. This pattern is clearly seen in how Jesus trained His disciples. Although He began with giving them simple acts of service to perform, He gradually increased their responsibilities. He sent them out on their own to minister and gave them positions of leadership within the larger band of followers.

Growth in faith and trust in Christ (Proverbs 3:5-6)

A further area of equipping is growth in our willingness and ability to exercise faith and trust in Christ. Growth in faith means growing in strength of conviction and quickness to obey. Simply put, it means putting into action what we believe to be true. In fact, the putting into action is the proof that we truly do believe something to be so.

Some years ago, there was a tightrope walker who performed unbelievable feats high above the ground. A promoter offered him a substantial sum of money to walk a tightrope across Niagara Falls. The event drew large crowds of people, eager to see the daring (or folly) of this artist. When the moment came, the performer calmly walked above the rushing waters, to the wild cheers of the crowd. Then he walked across blindfolded. The cheers grew even louder. It appeared that the show was over, but the artist had one act left to perform. He had a wheelbarrow raised to the rope and asked the crowd if they believed he could walk the wheelbarrow across the falls. The crowd responded enthusiastically. Then he asked for a volunteer to get into the wheelbarrow, and the crowd fell silent. All had said they believed, but none was willing to act on that belief. As Christians, we demonstrate our faith by a ready willingness to "get into the wheelbarrow."

> To really know God in this personal, real way, a believer must interact daily with Him and His Word and put the Truth into action.

Growth in trust means applying our faith in more and more areas. It is one thing to recognize Christ as our only way of salvation and place our trust in Him as Savior. It is quite another to begin to trust Him in all areas of our lives. After all, we have grown up learning to be independent and to trust in ourselves— our knowledge, our abilities, and so on. However, as the writer of Proverbs reminds us, we need to trust in the Lord with all our hearts and not lean on our own understanding (Proverbs 3:5). Admittedly, this is hard to do. But it is an important part of the maturing process. God, in His wisdom and providence, continues to bring circumstances into our lives that give us opportunities to trust Him and expand our faith. As we encounter these circumstances, God provides the resources to deal with them, as we take a risk and trust Him.

It seems that God sometimes gets us into tough situations just so we can learn to trust Him. The Bible certainly provides enough examples, whether it be Abraham standing over Isaac on the altar, the Israelites huddled on the banks of the Red Sea with the Egyptians in fierce pursuit, Daniel's friends in the fiery furnace, Jesus' disciples fighting a raging storm on the Sea of Galilee, or any number of other events. One of the most important things that every Christian must learn is that God can be trusted, regardless of circumstances that would make it appear otherwise.

THE RESTORING DIMENSION INVOLVES DEVELOPING EMOTIONAL AND RELATIONAL HEALTH.

As was mentioned earlier, it is critical that we also give attention to the restoring dimension of a believer's life as well as the equipping dimension. Spiritual growth will not occur in many areas unless there is maturity in the restorative areas discussed below.

We need to develop emotional health.

Developing emotional health begins with learning to think correctly, because emotions are a natural response to our thinking about, or interpretation of, the things that happen around us or to us. Thinking correctly involves both what we think (content) and how we think (process). Incorrect thinking is often based on an incorrect or inadequate view of ourselves, of others, or of God. These viewpoints or perspectives are largely formed in childhood and are influenced by the people and events closest to us. It is critical that we learn to counter falsehood with truth.

Consider the following example: A student receives a "B" on a test instead of the expected "A" and feels worthless. The "worthless" feeling is the content of her thinking. She arrived at this content, or conclusion, by the following thought process (beliefs that led to the student's conclusion). First, "I must always be perfect in order to be valuable." Second, "I made a mistake, and therefore I am not perfect." Third, "Therefore, I am not valuable. I am worthless." Both the content and the process need to be corrected. The key is to be able to identify where one's thinking goes wrong or, to put it another way, to identify which proposition is not true. In the example above, the second phrase is true (she did make mistakes; she is not perfect), while the first and third are not. The student's thought process starts on a false premise and inevitably ends with a false conclusion.

Along with learning to develop right thinking, we need to develop certain emotional skills if we are to achieve emotional health. These skills include learning to process emotions in the present and learning to process emotions that have been buried.

> ...emotions are a natural response to our thinking about, or interpretations of, the things that happen around us or to us.

We learn to process emotions in the present by being able to identify how we feel and express those feelings, even if they are unpleasant. It is often helpful to talk about your emotions with a trusted friend. Use words that describe how you feel. Say, "I feel…angry, sad, anxious, confused, embarrassed, secure, happy, relieved, daring." Be as specific as you can and don't use a "weaker" or "safer" word when a "stronger" one is appropriate. If someone has offended you, you may need to talk about your emotions in a controlled way with that person. Once you have processed your emotions, you need to release those that are negative. This release may mean choosing to forgive, if someone has offended or wronged you.

We need to develop relational health.

Developing emotional health rightly precedes a discussion of developing relational health, because relational health is impossible for a person who has not achieved at least some measure of personal emotional health. In order to be able to relate to another person in a mature, healthy way, you must first understand and be able to manage your own emotions. Or, to put it another way, until you are comfortable in your own skin, you are unlikely to feel comfortable around other people or unlikely to make them feel comfortable around you.

Skills necessary for relational health include the following:

- *Developing intimacy.* Intimacy is the ability to connect with another person at a deep level. This involves sharing thoughts and feelings about yourself.

- *Setting boundaries.* Boundaries are limits, or markers, that define a person as separate from others and help define what is unique about that person. Boundaries define what a person is, what he chooses, what he feels, what he likes, what he wants, and so on. A person needs to set his own boundaries and not allow others to set them for him.

- *Developing good communication skills.* These skills include speaking clearly, listening carefully, and giving constructive feedback.

CONCLUSION

It is critical to a person's spiritual growth that she develops both the equipping and restorative (emotional and relational) dimensions of her life. Spiritual growth is a life-long process. The important thing is to stay on the path and continue the journey. The good news is that these various dimensions of our being have a positive relationship to one another. As we grow in our knowledge of God, in service and in faith and trust, it will help us to grow emotionally and relationally. And as we grow emotionally and relationally, it will help us to grow in our relationship with God and service to Him. It is important to remember this truth—"He who began a good work in you will carry it on to completion." (Philippians 1:6)

The Restoring Dimension Of Spiritual Growth

DEVELOPING EMOTIONAL HEALTH

A. Develop right thinking.

1. Emotions are a natural response to our thinking about or interpretation of life. Therefore, it is critical that we learn to think correctly.

2. Thinking correctly involves both content ("what I think") and process ("how I think").
   Example: Situation: A student has received a "B" on a test.
   Content of thinking: "I am worthless."
   Process of thinking: (beliefs that led to the student's conclusion)
   First, "I must always be perfect in order to be valuable."
   Second, "I made a mistake, and therefore I am not perfect."
   Third, "Therefore, I am not valuable. I am worthless."

B. Develop emotional skills.

1. Learn to process emotions in the present.
   a. Identify your emotions.
   b. Talk about your emotions with a trusted friend. Use words that describe how you feel, "I feel...angry, sad, anxious, confused, embarrassed, secure, happy, relieved, daring."
   c. If someone has offended you, you may need to talk about your emotions in a controlled way with that person.
   d. Release the emotions. (Choose to forgive, if necessary.)

2. Learn to process emotions that have been buried.
   a. To deal with buried emotions, remember the unresolved, painful situations and allow the emotions to surface.
   b. If emotions do not surface, you may need to seek help from someone who understands emotional issues (e.g. counselor, restorative group).
   c. After emotions have surfaced, use the process outlined above for dealing with emotions in the present.

3. Some people "get stuck" at some point in this process and may need to seek outside help to complete the process.

DEVELOPING RELATIONAL HEALTH

A. Develop intimacy. Intimacy is the ability to connect with another person at a deep level. This involves sharing thoughts and feelings about yourself.

B. Set boundaries.

1. Boundaries are limits, or markers, that define a person as separate from others.

2. Boundaries define what a person is, what he chooses, what he feels, what he likes, what he wants, etc. Boundaries help define what is unique about a person.

3. A person needs to set her own boundaries and not allow others to set them for her.

C. Develop good communication skills.

1. Speak clearly.

2. Listen carefully.

3. Give constructive feedback.

Dimensions Of Spiritual Growth

IMPORTANT to Leader: Answers and notes to leaders are in gray, italicized text.

GOALS:

For a disciple to understand the two dimensions of spiritual growth: equipping and restoring.

For a disciple to make appropriate application of these dimensions to her life.

GETTING STARTED:

Think about this: how would it affect a person's life if she only ate food from one of the food groups?

Would miss nutrients from other foods and would be malnourished.

Transition: For a Christian to grow spiritually in a healthy way, several areas of growth need to be addressed. These areas fall into two larger categories: equipping and restoring.

STUDYING TOGETHER:

EQUIPPING GROWTH

Read Luke 5:1-11.

1. In this passage, how did Jesus' disciples grow in their knowledge of God and faith as a result of the experience?

   a) Peter realized that his heart was sinful, and that sin separated him from Jesus (God).
   b) Peter was amazed and humbled when he saw Jesus' command over nature and grew in his understanding of who Jesus was.
   c) Peter (and his friends) came to a point where they wanted to pursue Christ more than their livelihoods.

2. How did Peter use his skills and abilities to further the ministry of Jesus?

   He made his boat and his skills in maneuvering it available. Again, this was to help Jesus further His goals (the Father's goals).

3. What did Jesus say to encourage Peter (and the other disciples) about his future in God's Kingdom?

In spite of Peter's flaws (sins), Jesus told him that he would "fish for people." That is, He would bring people into the Kingdom.

RESTORING GROWTH

Growing in Christlikeness is more than growing in knowledge, skills and trust (equipping). It also includes growing in emotional and relational abilities (restoring growth). Often restoring growth requires healing of emotions and/or relationships.

Read Isaiah 61:1-2.

4. Jesus quotes this passage in Luke 4:18-21, and says that His ministry will include the healing (emotional and relational) for those who are rejected and damaged by society.

Read Exhibit entitled *The Restoring Dimension Of Growth.*

Then, read the following Case Study.

Ralph is a middle-aged businessman who is married with 2 children. His job is demanding, and he works at least 70+ hours/week. He says that when he is at work he feels fulfilled and important, but when he's at home he feels frustrated, unimportant, and often angry. He tells friends at work that he dreads the thought of going home. He knows there will be loud fights with his wife over his being late, his lack of involvement with the children and how lonely and isolated she feels because even when he's home, he does nothing more than watch TV. She complains that he doesn't communicate with her.

Ralph grew up in a home with an alcoholic father and an emotionally distant mother who tried to pretend that everything (even her husband's drinking) was OK. His dad was a hard worker at his job and made a good living for the family. He was able to compartmentalize his drinking so that it didn't interfere with work. His involvement with his children was minimal and usually consisted of an occasional family outing. The relationship between Ralph's father and mother was not all bad. At times (the rare times his father wasn't drinking), they enjoyed each other. But most of the time they fought about money, the house, the kids, etc.

5. List ways that you see Ralph struggling with issues mentioned in the Exhibit.

Wrong Thinking:

- *"My work needs me and my family doesn't (except as a provider)."*
- *"My work defines who I am; my significance comes from my work."*
- *"My childhood and my family were healthy, was the standard."*
- *"There is no hope that things at home will ever change."*

Emotional Skills:

- *Ralph feels angry, but doesn't know how to talk about his anger in an appropriate way.*
- *He avoids dealing with emotions (his and his wife's) by working.*
- *He avoids negative emotions associated with his family (wife and children).*

Relational Skills:

- Intimacy: *Ralph isn't able to connect with his wife.*
- Boundaries:
  - *He doesn't know how to set boundaries at work; how to control work so it doesn't interfere with home.*
  - *Chooses to work late; doesn't set boundaries for himself.*
- Communication:
  - *He doesn't express himself well about how he is feeling.*
  - *Doesn't listen to his wife.*

6. How might the home he grew up in contribute to Ralph's current problems?

- *His parents provided no model of how to talk about emotions in a healthy way.*
- *Parents didn't model healthy emotional connections within the family (intimacy).*
- *Father modeled avoidance by drinking. Ralph learned the lesson and avoided difficult situations by being a workaholic.*
- *Father modeled emotional neglect of his children, and Ralph does the same.*
- *His parents modeled poor communication in their personal relationship, and Ralph and his wife do the same.*

LOOKING AT REAL LIFE:

7. What are some benefits of developing healthy emotional and relational skills?

    - *Closer relationships*
    - *More self-aware and feel better about self*
    - *More helpful and understanding to those who are struggling*
    - *Better relationship with God; able to grow more spiritually*
    - *Are able to be helpful to someone without getting unduly entangled in their problem(s) (i.e. able to set boundaries)*
    - *Have better judgment about people, schedules, etc.*

LOOKING AT MY LIFE:

Which one of these skills do you think you need to grow in?

Ask God to show you what the next step should be for you?

Share with each other about your need for growth, and pray for each other.

Roles In Spiritual Growth

"God, make me good, but not yet." —St. Augustine

The quote above attributed to one of the early church fathers, while perhaps tongue in cheek, contains a significant element of truth. Our goodness (growth in holiness) depends on God, but it also depends on us. God will not make us good until we are ready and willing to partner with Him in the process.

Some Christians see spiritual growth as primarily God's responsibility, while others believe that spiritual growth is primarily a person's responsibility. The truth is that both God and people are involved in spiritual growth, and there is a balance or tension between the two roles. There are many verses in the Bible that speak to each role: I Peter 2:2; Ephesians 1:4; Romans 8:29.

And, it is also clear in the Word that there is tension between the two roles. Paul provides remarkable insight into this complementary dynamic when he writes in Colossians 1:29, "To this end I labor, struggling with all His energy, which so powerfully works in me." Paul was aware that he had a responsibility to expend effort; however, he also recognized that, without God working through him and giving him strength, his efforts would come to nothing. Philippians 2:12-13 also reflects both the obedience of the believer and the work of God. It is the interaction between what God does and what we do that produces growth.

> It is the interaction between what God does and what we do that produces growth.

Consider, for example, the building of a garden shed. You may think about what you want the shed to look like, and draft plans for the structure. You may even secure all the necessary tools and materials to build the shed. However, at some point you have to actually get to work—to saw boards and hammer nails—or the shed will never get built. Successful completion doesn't depend on your grand dreams or your good intentions. It comes about only through hard work. So it is with the Christian life. God has placed everything we need for growth at our disposal but, until we actually start to use what we have been given, we will not make progress. We can better understand spiritual growth when we understand the differences between God's role and our role.

GOD'S ROLE IN SPIRITUAL GROWTH

God influences us inwardly, through the Holy Spirit.

God's internal influence in our spiritual growth takes place primarily through the work of the Holy Spirit living in us. At the time of salvation, the Holy Spirit comes to reside in our lives permanently. Speaking to this point, Paul challenged the believers at Rome: "You, however, are controlled not by the sinful nature but by the Spirit, if the Spirit of God lives in you. And if anyone does not have the Spirit of Christ, they do not belong to Christ." (Romans 8:9) This indwelling of the Spirit is the basis of all else that happens in our spiritual lives.

The Holy Spirit produces a permanent change of heart that causes the believer's disposition to be tender toward God instead of hostile toward Him (Romans 8:5-8). The Old Testament prophet Ezekiel spoke of this heart transplant as God taking away hearts of stone and giving hearts of flesh (Ezekiel 11:19). He went on to say that, after surgery, the transplant recipients would follow God's decrees and be careful to keep His laws.

As we yield ourselves to God and obey Him, His Spirit impacts us in many ways. He gives us holy desires. Along with writing God's law on our hearts, the Spirit also grants us the desire to follow what God's law tells us to do. As Paul explained to the Galatians, "For the sinful nature desires what is contrary to the Spirit, and the Spirit what is contrary to the sinful nature. They are in conflict with each other, so that you do not do what you want." (Galatians 5:17) In other words, though we still have to battle against our sin nature that wants us to continue in sin, we now have the Holy Spirit leading us to pursue righteousness.

> The Spirit also grants us the desire to follow what God's law tells us to do.

God through the Holy Spirit also gives us power—power to walk in obedience, power to do good works (Ephesians 3:20), power to stand against evil (Ephesians 6:10), power to stand up under adversity (II Corinthians 12:10), and power to bear witness before an unbelieving world (Acts 1:8 and 4:33).

God also works by convicting us of sin (John 16:8-11). In the devotional booklet *Our Daily Bread*, the story is told of a young girl who accepted Christ as her Savior and applied for membership in a local church. "Were you a sinner before you received the Lord Jesus into your life?" inquired an old deacon. "Yes, sir," she replied. "Well, are you still a sinner?" "To tell you the truth, I feel I'm a greater sinner than ever." "Then what real change have you experienced?" "I don't quite know how to explain it," she said, "except I used to be a sinner running after sin, but now that I am saved I'm a sinner running from sin!" She was received into the fellowship of the church, and she proved by her consistent life that she was truly converted.

The girl's words in this story, "I feel I'm a greater sinner than ever," ring true with many Christians who are experiencing spiritual growth. This greater awareness of sin occurs because the Spirit reveals more and more sin to us. As we pray with the psalmist, "Search me, O God, and know my heart...see if there is any offensive way in me," the Spirit will point out to us areas that we still need to work on. Whenever we become aware of sin, we recognize that the Spirit is doing His job.

A final impact of God's Spirit on us is that He writes His law on our hearts. God, speaking through His prophet Jeremiah, foretold the day when He would make a new covenant with His people (through the death and resurrection of Jesus Christ). He said, "I will put my laws in their minds, and I will write them on their hearts." (Jeremiah 31:33, *New Living Translation*) This new covenant would not be written on tablets of stone but would rather be engraved on hearts by the Holy Spirit. Even today we contrast the phrase "the letter of the law" with "the spirit of the law."

The religious leaders of Jesus' day knew the law down to the letter. However, it had not been written on their hearts. As a result, Jesus would say of them, "You are like whitewashed tombs, which look beautiful on the outside but on the inside are full of dead men's bones." (Matthew 23:27) Elsewhere, quoting the words of the prophet Isaiah, Jesus charged the religious leaders saying, "These people honor me with their lips, but their hearts are far from me." (Matthew 15:8) It is only when God's Spirit writes His law on our hearts that we can worship Him in spirit and in truth.

God also influences us outwardly.

God uses difficult circumstances, consequences of our choices, and persecution to cause us to grow spiritually. Responding appropriately to unfavorable events or circumstances is a frequent theme in Scripture. The first letter to the Thessalonians tells believers to give thanks in all circumstances (I Thessalonians 5:18). This is not a fatalistic mind-set; rather, it represents a mature understanding of the greater purposes that can be achieved through these tribulations. As we endure suffering, we remain confident that God causes everything to work together for good for those who love Him (Romans 8:28). The writer of Hebrews tells us that God's discipline is not whimsical. He disciplines us for our own good, in order to make us holy (Hebrews 12:7-11). In the Old Testament, Joseph acknowledged his understanding of this principle concerning the persecution from his brothers: "You intended to harm me, but God intended it for good to accomplish what is now being done, the saving of many lives." (Genesis 50:20)

As we exercise these spiritual disciplines, God brings about growth in our lives.

God also uses positive results from our walk with God to motivate us to continue our pursuit of holiness. We are told in Scripture to obey God, to spend time with Him in prayer, to study His Word, to serve others, etc. As we exercise these spiritual disciplines, God brings about growth in our lives. When we engage in healthy activities such as proper diet, rest, and exercise, we feel better and this motivates us to continue. So it is with the spiritual life. The more we grow, the more we desire to grow. In His last meal with His disciples Jesus tells them that if they maintain a close relationship with Him (through the Holy Spirit after Pentecost), they will be fruitful in character and in ministry (John 15:5,7-8). He also assures them that if they are obedient to Him, He will reveal Himself to them (John 14:21). In the fifth chapter Paul tells the Galatians that if they are faithful to live by the Spirit ("keep in step with the Spirit"), their lives will reflect God's character (Galatians 5:16,22-25).

Understanding God's role in our spiritual growth (both inwardly and outwardly) leads us to a position of humility, gratitude and dependence. Further, a deep understanding of God's ongoing work of grace in our lives should motivate us to take responsibility for the role we play in our own growth, which is discussed next.

MANKIND'S ROLE IN SPIRITUAL GROWTH

God gives many instructions to believers about what they should do to grow spiritually. A word of caution as we delve into this topic. The Christian life is a marathon rather than a sprint. It takes time to develop the endurance necessary to run a marathon. Some believers hear of great Christian saints who read many chapters of the Bible or pray for several hours each day. Inspired by their example and determined to imitate their dedication, they try to maintain the same habits. Rare is the person who can immediately achieve that level of discipline. Most of us never do. And that's okay. As we will see below, God does call us to study His Word and to pray. But it is far better to start slowly and develop.

Following God's instructions is not always easy, but the fruit is of great value.

Having said this, the degree to which a believer follows God's instructions influences the degree to which he grows. Following God's instructions is not always easy, but the fruit is of great value. As the believer engages in the following activities, he will grow spiritually.

Understand and apply the Word of God.

As believers we grow spiritually as we get to know God—His nature, His purposes, and His ways. And the Bible is the primary source God uses to reveal Himself to us. In order to get to know God better, a believer must come to understand the meaning of Scripture by hearing, reading, studying, memorizing and meditating on the Word. In his second letter to Timothy, Paul writes of the importance and value of Scripture in these words, "All Scripture is inspired by God and is useful to teach us what is true and to make us realize what is wrong in our lives. It straightens us out and teaches us to do what is right. It is God's way of preparing us in every way, fully equipped for every good thing God wants us to do." (II Timothy 3:16-17, *New Living Translation*)

It is important that our study of the Word never becomes an end in itself. The purpose of study is to learn and to grow, not just to gain more knowledge. There are people who know much about the Bible and have even memorized lengthy passages but do not believe in the God of the Bible and have no interest in obeying Him. James warned his readers against being hearers of the Word only, saying that in so doing they were deceiving themselves (James 1:22).

Pray.

God has provided an open line of communication with believers through prayer. Prayer is simply talking to God, knowing that He is always available to communicate with us, and expecting Him to respond to us in the way that best suits His purposes and our best interests. However, prayer is not simply an option that we should resort to when we have exhausted our own resources. Rather it should be the natural response to any situation we find ourselves in. We should turn to God first, whether to ask for guidance, protection, provision, or whatever need we might have. Ephesians 6:18 tells us to "pray in the Spirit on all occasions with all kinds of prayers and requests."

Fellowship with believers.

One of the greatest needs of our day is for people to develop healthy relationships. God knows this and has provided for this need through fellowship with other believers through the church. The restoration of our vertical relationship with God paves the way for healthy, mutually beneficial horizontal relationships with others. However, these relationships must be nourished through spending time together and celebrating the life we share in Jesus.

This is why Scripture tells us that we should not neglect meeting together with other believers (Hebrews 10:24-25). We need each other. The Christian life was never designed to be an individual pursuit. Regular fellowship with other believers provides comfort, accountability, instruction, encouragement, support, and direction. If a believer is not involved in a local church, she may develop distorted thinking, lack emotional support, feel insecure, and flounder without accountability.

Serve others.

Not only are we to spend time with other believers, we are to serve one another. Again, Jesus is our example. He told His disciples that He came not to be served but rather to serve others. Later He challenged them to serve others as He had served them (Matthew 20:28 and John 13:15).

Serving others is not simply something God thought up to help build character. Rather, service benefits both the giver and the receiver. It benefits the receiver by meeting a need. It benefits the giver by allowing him to experience the joy of seeing a need met and by enabling him to impact others. Along the way, we all have the opportunity to be on the giving end and on the receiving end, and we can find equal joy in each.

Most service to others is nothing heroic, but simply involves everyday expressions of love such as offering a kind word of encouragement, giving someone a ride, providing a listening ear, fixing a meal, having a good attitude, or sharing what God is doing in our lives. Scripture emphasizes the "everydayness" of service by saying, "Whenever we have the opportunity, we should do good to everyone, especially to our Christian brothers and sisters." (Galatians 6:10, *New Living Translation*)

CONCLUSION

Christians grow spiritually when they are faithful to complete the responsibilities of the role God has given them. The four responsibilities covered in this Pocket Principle™ (understand and apply the Word of God, pray, fellowship with other believers and serve others) do not exhaust the opportunities a Christian has for growth. Other disciplines that may prove helpful to the believer include silence, solitude, fasting and frugality among others.

God reminds us that He is always faithful to carry out His role in our growth. In Philippians 1:6 Paul says, "He who began a good work in you will carry it on to completion until the day of Jesus Christ." This knowledge of God's role in our spiritual growth leads us to a position of humility, gratitude and dependence. A deep understanding of God's ongoing work of grace in our lives should motivate us to take responsibility for the role we play in our growth and energize us for the task.

Roles In Spiritual Growth

IMPORTANT to Leader: Answers and notes to leaders are in gray, italicized text.

GOALS:

For a disciple to understand that both God and the believer have responsibility in spiritual growth.

For a disciple to identify how this principle has worked in his spiritual life in the past (i.e. to focus on a situation in which the disciple can identify what his responsibility was and what God's responsibility was).

GETTING STARTED:

What do you think the responsible parent's role and the child's role are in the following situations?

1) A 12-year-old child is failing a class because homework hasn't been turned in.

2) A 17-year-old child must have a summer job (needs funds for college).

Transition: While we may not all agree on exactly what each person's role is, it is clear that each person in the situation has responsibilities to carry out. In today's lesson, we will study our role and God's role in our spiritual growth.

STUDYING TOGETHER:

Read Colossians 1:28-29.

1. What was Paul's role in the spiritual development of believers?

   He proclaimed Christ, admonished, taught, labored and struggled.

2. What was God's role in the spiritual development of believers?

   God supplied to Paul His supernatural energy that worked powerfully in Paul's life as he labored and struggled to see spiritual growth take place in the lives of believers.

3. Can you remember a time when you knew the Holy Spirit was working through your actions? What were the results?

Read Philippians 2:12-13.

4. According to verse 13, what role does God play in our spiritual development?

   God works through His Holy Spirit to give us the right desires (to will) and the strength to live out (to act) His purposes in our lives.

5. According to verse 12, what is our responsibility in our own spiritual maturing?

   We are to make every effort (to work out) to grow in Christ. In doing so, we should do it with fear and trembling, trusting in God's power to help us.

6. Identify the believer's responsibility and God's responsibility in the following biblical examples:

   Exodus 17:8-13

   Believer's Responsibility—*Moses was to hold up the staff; Joshua led battle; Aaron and Hur held up Moses' arms.*

   God's Responsibility—*God empowered the Israelites to overcome the Amalekites in battle.*

   Luke 18:1-7

   Believer's Responsibility—*Keep praying and never give up.*

   God's Responsibility—*God would answer the prayer in His timing and wisdom.*

Acts 8:26-39

Believer's Responsibility—*Philip obeyed the command to go; Philip witnessed to and baptized Ethiopian; Ethiopian decided to be baptized.*

God's Responsibility—*Directed through angel and Spirit; took Philip away; worked in the Ethiopian's heart.*

LOOKING AT REAL LIFE:

The Growth Responsibility Scale

I'm totally responsible   We're both responsible   God's totally responsible

```
|_____|_____|
```

7. What are some of the positive and negative aspects associated with a Christian believing he is totally responsible for his spiritual growth?

   Positive—*Possible answers: discipline, desire*

   Negative—*Possible answers: legalism, get tired, frustration, guilt, stress*

8. What are some of the positive and negative aspects associated with a Christian believing God is totally responsible for his spiritual growth?

   Positive—*Possible answers: peace, humility*

   Negative—*Possible answers: laziness, lack of discipline, lack of passion*

9. What are some of the positive and negative aspects associated with a Christian believing that he and God both have a responsibility in his spiritual growth?

   Positive—*Possible answers: faith that produces works, obedience, love in action*

   Negative—*none*

LOOKING AT MY LIFE:

Can you think of a time in your spiritual development where you really saw a spiritual breakthrough in your life? What role did God play? What role did you play?

What area in your spiritual development has hit a snag? What can you do to move forward and grow in that area? What will God need to do through you or in you in order for that to happen?

Close in prayer, thanking God for His work on your behalf to make you more like Christ. Then, ask Him to give you the desire and strength to grow in the area that you listed in the question above.

The Filling Of The Holy Spirit

"The average church member's understanding of the Holy Spirit is so vague it is nearly non-existent."
(source unknown)

It is important for Christians to understand the person and work of the Holy Spirit and how they can follow Scripture's command to be filled with the Spirit. Not only is the Holy Spirit an equal person of the triune Godhead, worthy of our worship and obedience, but also, His ministry is of utmost importance in our lives. In fact, Jesus told His disciples that it was good for them that He go away so that He could send the Spirit (John 16:7). What an incredible thought this must have been to the disciples, who were fearful and full of grief because Jesus was talking about leaving them. But obviously, He meant what He said.

The Holy Spirit is instrumental in the process of salvation. The Spirit brings conviction to our hearts and shows us our need of a Savior. Jesus describes the new birth as being born of the Spirit (John 3:6). At salvation, the Holy Spirit comes to dwell in the believer and is the defining characteristic that he is truly a believer. Paul writes that those who do not have the Spirit of Christ living in them are not Christians at all (Romans 8:9). By contrast, Paul says that those who truly are Christians are marked with a seal, who is the Holy Spirit (Ephesians 1:13). John echoes this thought when he writes, "We know that we live in Him and He in us, because He has given us of His Spirit." (I John 4:13)

> Our entire Christian life should be characterized by a continual reliance on the Spirit.

However, the work of the Spirit is not limited to our initial conversion experience. Scripture emphasizes the importance for every believer to be filled with the Spirit. Our entire Christian life should be characterized by a continual reliance on the Spirit. "Walk in the Spirit" is a constant refrain of the New Testament epistles, letters that were written to give instruction to the early Christians. Alternate phrases such as "living by faith," "drawing near to God," and "submitting to God," relate to this same idea of being filled with the Spirit.

In Scripture the phrase "filling of the Spirit" is used to describe the empowering, wisdom, and guidance the Spirit brings into a believer's life. Just before returning to heaven, Jesus told His disciples that the Holy Spirit would soon come and give them power—power that would enable them to be His witnesses (Acts 1:8). When the Holy Spirit did come upon the believers on the day of Pentecost, He filled them with power, with the result that they lived holy lives and impacted the community. Let's look at the command in Ephesians 5:18 to "be filled with the Spirit."

"TO BE FILLED"

The complex verb structure of Ephesians 5:18 needs to be explored to better understand the Holy Spirit. There are four parts to the verb structure in this verse. The English translation is unable to reflect all the facets of the original Greek, so we need to study this verb in some detail. The following four points provide further insight.

Command: The filling is a command.

In Ephesians 5:18 Paul commands the believers at Ephesus to be filled with the Spirit. This command shows that it is God's will for believers to be filled with the Spirit. It is not an option; it is imperative to the Christian lifestyle. A scuba instructor would never tell a student, "The oxygen tank you have strapped to your back is your source of life. When you go under water, you can open the valve if you so desire." Rather, he would command, "You must open the valve to your tank when you go underwater. It is the only way you can survive." For a believer to attempt to live the Christian life without the filling of the Spirit is as foolish as it would be for a scuba diver to attempt to go deep under water without opening the valve to her air tank.

> The Spirit also grants us the desire to follow what God's law tells us to do.

Plural: The command applies to all believers.

The understood subject "you" in Ephesians 5:18 is plural. The plural subject shows that the command was written to the whole church and not just to a particular person or to a select group of individuals. This command applies to all believers, young or old, male or female, introverted or extroverted, immature or mature. Being filled with the Spirit cannot be equated with maturity in Christ; however, it is a key part of the maturing process. We could perhaps say that one can be filled with the Spirit without being mature, but no one can reach Christian maturity without the consistent work of the Spirit in his life.

Passive Mood: The filling is not done by us.

The verb is in the passive mood. When "be filled" is translated in the passive mood, it reads, "let the Spirit fill you." In other words, it is something God wants to do for us. It is not something that requires us to meet difficult conditions first (other than submitting to His lordship, which can be difficult indeed). We do not need to achieve a certain level of expertise, we do not need to acquire certain knowledge or to learn special techniques—we simply need to let God fill us with His Spirit.

Present Tense: The filling needs to be an ongoing process.

The verb is in the present tense. In the Greek language, the present tense often conveys the idea that the action of the verb is repeated again and again. Thus, the filling of the Spirit needs to continually be made a reality through conscious dependence on God. The moment we choose to resume control over our own lives (when our feelings get hurt, when we get pushed into a corner, when we decide we want something we shouldn't have or for whatever reason), we are no longer filled (under the control of) the Spirit.

In this Pocket Principle™ we are discussing more about what it means to be filled with the Spirit, but there is a mysterious aspect of being filled that cannot be explained. In the third chapter of his gospel account, John captures a conversation between Jesus and Nicodemus, who was a religious leader of the Jews. Jesus was discussing

This command shows that it is God's will for believers to be filled with the Spirit.

the necessity of the new birth and, in this context, He said, "The wind blows wherever it pleases. You hear its sound, but you cannot tell where it comes from or where it is going. So it is with everyone born of the Spirit." (John 3:8) Just as there is a mystical element to the Spirit's work in salvation, so too there is a mysterious element to the Spirit's ongoing work in our lives that cannot be fully explained. However, we can begin to understand how a person is filled with the Spirit by understanding two biblical principles: drawing near to God and submitting to God.

DRAWING NEAR TO GOD (JOHN 7:37-39)

In its essence, Christianity is a relationship with Christ. When Christ called the first disciples to come and follow Him, He was calling them into a relationship with Him. The same is true of all who follow Him today. Through the miracle of the new birth into the family of God, we enter a new relationship. The Christian life is an unfolding, a widening, and a deepening of that relationship. Everything concerning Christian growth has its foundation in this relationship. Therefore, the filling of the Holy Spirit grows out of our relationship with Jesus.

John 7:37-39 emphasizes the connection between the filling of the Spirit and our relationship with Christ.

On the last and greatest day of the Feast, Jesus stood and said in a loud voice, "Let anyone who is thirsty come to me and drink. Whoever believes in me, as the Scripture has said, rivers of living water will flow from within them." By this He meant the Spirit, whom those who believed in Him were later to receive. Up to that time the Spirit had not been given, since Jesus had not yet been glorified.

Verse 39 indicates that Jesus was preparing believers for the time after His death when the Holy Spirit would come and continue His ministry. When Jesus talks about a relationship with Himself, He is also talking about the filling of the Holy Spirit. Jesus invites believers to be filled with the Holy Spirit by relating to Him as indicated by the three action verbs recorded in John 7:37-39. These actions are discussed below.

"Come to me."

Thirst is a gift from the Creator. Just as physical thirst is a signal that our body needs refreshment, so our spiritual thirst points out a need. Becoming aware of our spiritual thirst motivates us to come to Jesus. However, many go through life dissatisfied, discouraged, and despondent, but totally unaware of their thirst. It was no different in Jesus' day.

In order to quench this deep thirst of our souls, we must come to Jesus. Nothing else and no one else can satisfy. The verb "come" in this passage is continuous, which means we are to "come to Jesus" again and again. Thus, spiritual thirst, like physical thirst, must be satisfied repeatedly. This truth reminds us that spiritual thirst is present both before and after salvation. Although Christians enjoy a relationship with God, this relationship is still hampered by our sinfulness and by living in a fallen world.

Note that Jesus invites us to come, but He does not coerce us. He does not force His way into our lives but rather offers us the opportunity to come enjoy His life. This stance is true to His nature and true to His design in creating us as moral beings. He pursues us passionately and yearns for us to respond to Him. The "inviting" nature of God is woven throughout Scripture.

"Drink of Me."

After coming to Jesus, we must "drink" of Him. This verb also indicates an often-repeated action, a frequent or continual coming to Him to drink. We drink of Jesus by engaging in relational activities such as the following:

- Communing with Him—that is, simply dwelling in His presence and spending time with Him

- Worshipping Him—telling God how wonderful He is, reflecting on His marvelous deeds, expressing appreciation for who He is and all that He has done for us

- Listening to Him—reading His Word, being quiet before Him, trying to discern the leading of His Spirit

- Casting our cares on Him—being open and honest before God about our needs, our hurts, and our desires, baring our soul to Him, telling Him everything we are concerned about

- Allowing Him to minister to us—letting His Spirit minister to our spirit, letting Him calm our fears, salve our wounds, and encourage our hearts

As we spend time with Jesus in these ways and enjoy our relationship with Him, we find that He quenches our spiritual thirst.

"Trust (believe) in me."

The third verb—believe—also expresses an action repeated over and over. We come to Jesus initially to trust Him to save us from our sins and to restore our relationship with God, which is our greatest need. Day by day, as we enjoy that restored relationship, Jesus invites us to choose to trust Him—to depend on Him to meet our needs.

Coming to Jesus, drinking of Him and trusting in Him is necessary for the believer to be filled to overflowing with the Spirit (v. 38).

SUBMITTING TO GOD

Another aspect to being filled with the Spirit is being submitted to God and to doing His will. It is very easy for us to turn away from God and go our own way even though we know that God's way is better. Or we may want to go God's way but try to do it in our own power. Either way we are not walking with God the way we should. The only way we can remain filled with the Spirit is by consciously submitting to God and looking to Him to strengthen and guide us.

The Scriptures use a couple of phrases to describe our disobedience. In Ephesians 4:30 we are told not to "grieve" the Holy Spirit. In that context Paul is admonishing believers to treat other people right. So doing wrong things, sins of commission, disrupts our relationship with the Holy Spirit. In I Thessalonians 5:19 Paul says don't "quench" the Holy Spirit. We quench the Holy Spirit by not continuing to follow Him or by trying to do some things in our own power. These sins are sometimes called sins of omission.

When we choose to go our own way, to disobey God, it becomes necessary to become filled with the Holy Spirit again. God does not make it difficult to get back on track. First, we need to confess and repent of what we have done. Confession means to "say the same thing as," to agree with the Holy Spirit that what we have done is wrong (I John 1:9). Repentance means to change our mind about sin and to turn away from it and toward God. When we turn to God, we need to consciously and willingly submit to Him and trust Him to fill us with the Holy Spirit again. He will do it because it is His will for us to be filled with the Holy Spirit. Although every Christian continues to struggle with sin, she will make progress against it as she grows; but the reality is that a believer will never completely be free of sin in this life.

SUMMARY

We should be filled with the Holy Spirit by drawing near to Christ daily and staying submitted to Him in all areas of life. When we are Spirit-filled we will increasingly become like Christ. Just a few of the characteristics of a believer who is walking with God (is filled with the Spirit) are mentioned here. The Spirit-filled believer exhibits the fruit of the Spirit in his life (Galatians 5:22), experiences answers to prayer, bears spiritual fruit (evangelism), is able to be a light to the dark world, and functions in a healthy way in the Body of Christ.

Spiritual Growth
The Filling Of The Holy Spirit

Guidelines for being filled with the Spirit:

- Draw near to God (John 7:37-39).

  - "Come to Me": Daily spend time with Him.

  - "Drink [of me]": Sit in His presence: communing with Him, casting your cares upon Him, listening to Him, worshipping Him and allowing Him to minister to you.

  - "Trust [believe] in Me": Choose to depend (trust, believe) on Him to meet your needs and to enable and empower you.

- Submit to God.

  - Ask God to bring to mind any sin(s) in your life or any areas He wants you to obey or trust Him in.

  - Write down whatever He brings to mind. Confess and repent.

  - Write I John 1:9 across the list of sin(s), and destroy the list.

  - Acknowledge your dependence on God (and submit to Him), and ask Him to fill you with His Spirit.

  - Believe that God wants to fill you with His Spirit and that He has.

The Filling Of The Holy Spirit

IMPORTANT to Leader: Answers and notes to leaders are in gray, italicized text.

GOALS:

For a disciple to understand that God wants all believers to be filled with the Spirit.

For a disciple to understand how to be filled with the Spirit.

GETTING STARTED:

There are many forms of fuel that produce power such as wind, gasoline, solar, etc. However, for any of them to work they must be accessed/harnessed. God has provided the Holy Spirit as a fuel (energy source) for us to use to live the Christian life. How do you think we can access this power?

Transition: Let's see how Scripture answers this question.

STUDYING TOGETHER:

BE FILLED.

Read Ephesians 5:18.

1. In this verse, what does God command for all believers to do?

    To "be filled with the Spirit."

    Note: The verb "be filled" is in the present tense. In the Greek language, this tense often conveys the idea that the action of the verb is repeated over and over. That is, "be filled" means to be filled again and again.

2. What does this verse tell you about the Spirit-filled life?

    a) Being filled is a command from God. b) Being filled with the Spirit is not just a one-time experience. It must occur over and over again in the believer's life. c) The analogy to wine suggests that we are to be controlled (drunk) by the Holy Spirit, not by wine, which represents anything else that may control us.

3. Why is this command important?

   Because as believers we need the Holy Spirit to successfully help us live the Christian life (Galatians 5:16).

DRAW NEAR TO GOD.

Read John 7:37-39.

4. What does Jesus invite the disciples to do, and what do you think it means?

   Come to me; drink and believe (trust)

   Note: All three of these verbs are in the present tense, and in this context, they mean that we are invited to do these things over and over.

5. Jesus uses the analogy of thirst to describe being filled with the Spirit. How is "thirst" like being filled with the Spirit?

   Thirst is necessary if we are to live physically (otherwise we might not drink), and we must drink spiritually or our spiritual life will suffer. Also, we need to drink over and over. We get filled (with water or the Spirit), but then need to drink again later.

6. What is the relationship between connecting with Christ and the filling of the Spirit?

   As we connect with Christ, our thirst for Him is satisfied. That is, we are filled with the Holy Spirit.

7. In verse 38 Jesus offers streams of living water (the Holy Spirit) flowing from within the believer. What is the implication of the fact that living water is flowing from within the believer?

   It should affect others around her; there should be an overflow to other people.

What do you think it looks like in a person's life if she has "rivers of living water" flowing from within her?

Read Galatians 5:22-23; John 15:7-8; Matthew 5:14-16.

8. According to these verses, what does it look like for a Christian to be filled with the Spirit (i.e. rivers of living water flowing from within her)?

   Fruit of the Spirit will be evident; will be answers to prayer; will be a light to the world.

SUBMIT TO GOD.

Read James 4:7.

9. According to James 4:7, why should we submit to God?

   To get out from under the influence of Satan.

Read Ephesians 4:29-32 and I Thessalonians 5:19-22.

10. How do we grieve (Ephesians 4:30) or quench (I Thessalonians 5:19) the Holy Spirit?

    We grieve or quench the Spirit when we consciously sin (when we don't submit to God.)

Read I John 1:9 and James 4:7-10.

11. When you realize that you have sinned, what should you do?

    Confess the sin, draw near to God, and submit your life to Christ.

LOOKING AT REAL LIFE:

12. What makes it difficult for a believer to stay submitted to God in all areas?

    Peer pressure, selfishness, worldly values, pride, stubbornness, etc.

LOOKING AT MY LIFE:

What makes it difficult for you to stay in fellowship with and submitted to God?
Share with the group if you feel comfortable doing so.

Pray for each other about what has been shared.

Leader: Instruct group members to read through the Exhibit entitled Spiritual
Growth—The Filling Of The Holy Spirit *on their own.*

7 Growing Through The Word And Prayer

I remember my first crush, Jenny, a 4th grade classmate. It was Valentine's Day. Swinging on the swing set I made up a song about her, and even created a special card. The problem was that I never talked to her! I thought the card would somehow magically cause her to notice me. But the results were disappointing; not much came from my efforts other than her saying "thank you" to me. Maybe I should have gotten the card with the candy attached!

The goal of Christianity is for every Christian to have a close, vibrant relationship with God. The good news is that God is much better at getting our attention than I was with my first crush. He has given us opportunities to get to know Him and for Him to communicate His love for us. We can read His "Love Letter" to us, the Bible, and talk to Him by praying. To continue to grow and have a healthy relationship with God a Christian must always take time to hear, read, memorize and meditate on God's Word and take time to listen and speak to Him in prayer.

GOD'S WORD

God's Word, the Bible, is one of the most important ways God speaks to believers. Some people rely on other methods to hear from God. Some look for inner peace or circumstances alone to point to God's will. I remember a student who was desperately trying to decide between two job offers and prayed that God would show him where he should work. When a car with a license plate from the state where one of the businesses was located passed, he concluded that that was a sign telling him to accept the job in that state. God can certainly give

> ...the first and most clear place we can hear from God is from His Word.

us signs, but the first and most clear place we can hear from God is from His Word. "All Scripture is breathed out by God and profitable for teaching, for reproof, for correction, and for training in righteousness, that the man of God may be complete, equipped for every good work." (II Timothy 3:16-17, *English Standard Version*) The Word of God is an objective check on other sources that claim to tell us about God and His will.

For the Christian, the Bible guides our lives and decisions by teaching us about God's character, how He works and the principles that support His Kingdom. He has given us an incredibly rich knowledge of who He is, what His will is and how to relate to Him (Psalm 19:7-11). There are many ways to take advantage of this richness: hearing, reading, studying, memorizing, and meditating on Scripture.

1. Hear. We hear God's Word as it is read and taught. A variety of settings (church service, Sunday School class, small group Bible study) provide opportunities to hear God's Word read aloud and taught.

2. Read. Taking time to read the Bible provides the believer with another opportunity to hear from God. There are a variety of ways to read Scripture. You may read larger portions of the Bible, using a reading plan that allows you to systematically read a variety of types of Biblical literature. Or you might slow the pace of your reading to allow time to consider the deeper meaning of phrases and words. Developing a daily, consistent time to read the Bible also nourishes your relationship with God as His Spirit shows you particular truths to apply to your life.

3. Study. Studying God's Word in more depth requires time and patience. Using a Study Bible or other tools can enhance Bible study. Finding a group to help you learn how to study the Bible is vitally important. WDA offers a resource to help people learn to study the Bible using an inductive Bible study method. It can be found on the WDA store on our website: www.disciplebuilding.org.

4. Meditate. It is also important to take time to slow down and meditate on Scripture. It reminds me of the way a child begins to lick and suck on a "tootsie pop," slowly twirling it in his mouth, savoring the sweet taste. It is wise to focus on an idea or a story from the Bible, asking yourself questions about it, taking time to define and clarify the meaning of words and phrases, and praying for a better understanding of how the Scripture applies to our lives, relates to others or teaches us about God.

5. Memorize. We are also told to "hide God's Word in our hearts." Knowing verses and passages of the Bible from memory provides the Christian with the knowledge necessary to apply God's Word to life, share the Word with others and find the protection and power to resist the temptations, lies and attacks that come from the evil one.

INTERPRETING GOD'S WORD

When we read God's Word, His Spirit opens our minds to understand Truth. We do, however, need to grow in our ability to interpret God's Word. There are many who dismiss God's Word because different Christians have different interpretations of the same passages. The challenge for the student of the Bible is to learn how to interpret correctly. Right interpretation of the Word isn't based on subjectivity or personal feelings. Sometimes people express their "feelings" about any particular subject, as if their feelings are an authoritative interpretation of a passage of Scripture. They are not.

> The challenge for the student of the Bible is to learn how to interpret correctly.

Instead, the Bible is our authority, and because of this, we are not to place ourselves as an authority over it. We need to understand that God has breathed His Word. The word "inspired" has a root meaning of *God-breathed*. God communicated His truth to the authors of each Biblical book in a way that used the original author's history, personality, and writing style. But at the same time, He guided the process so that all the words are "God breathed or inspired."

So, every passage in the Bible has only one correct interpretation, which is the meaning the original author intended for it to have. (It may be difficult to determine the correct interpretation of some passages, but this should not prevent us from diligently searching Scripture.) Some helpful resources are a Bible Dictionary, Bible Encyclopedia, and Expository Bible commentary. These can be found in Christian bookstores or on line. Richard Pratt, a seminary professor, theologian and author, has some helpful thoughts about understanding the author's meaning, looking at the context and then making application to our lives.

In his book, *He Gave Us Stories*, Pratt explains that we are to look at three things as we study a passage. First, we consider "That World," the particular story that is being told. An example would be looking at the story of Moses and the Nation of Israel crossing the Red Sea. "That World" is the scene that is being described in the text.

Second, we consider "Their World." This is the context of the audience of the book, the people to whom the book was given. So the original recipients were the Israelites during the 40 years they wandered in the Sinai Desert. We ask what Moses wanted to tell them in "their world."

Then we consider "Our World." After identifying That World, and Their World, we then ask, "How does this truth apply to the world in which we live?" By asking about *that* world, *their* world and *our* world and studying to find how they apply, we are learning how to interpret the Bible.

In our technological times, online resources and software are a rich source of information and help. Some resources are: www.logos.com and www.biblestudytools.com. If you use mobile devices you can find a variety of apps such as You Version, www.bible.com, www.logos.com/ipad and www.accordancebible.com/Accordance-For-IOS.

There will be disagreements.

There will be situations in which earnest, serious Christians disagree over the interpretation of God's Word. When this happens we must first remember that none of us are free from error. We are all relying on God to reveal His truth through His Word and Spirit. For this reason, I must hold my convictions with humility. We will not be able to resolve all disagreements, but my responsibility is to approach others with grace and love. Romans 12:18 calls the believer to "live at peace with everyone," and qualifies that command with the statement, "if it is possible." The goal of reading, studying and learning from God's Word is to be conformed into Christlikeness and to grow to maturity, not to win arguments or appear to be right. We have a great opportunity to learn from one another.

PRAYER

Open line of communication

God is available and willing to communicate with us. He responds to our humble prayers by revealing His truth in the Word, by prompting us with the Holy Spirit, by changing our hearts, and sometimes by being silent. Prayer is an important way to draw near to God (James 4:8) and be passionate about what is important to Him (Matthew 6:10).

Prayer changes us as we connect with God our Father; although it is tempting to think that prayer changes God. When we spend time in the Word and in prayer, God begins to align our desires and thoughts with His thoughts. Where we once prayed for our own wants and desires, we see our prayers come in line more and more with His desires!

Prayer can be a time to draw strength and wisdom from God, and also a time to pray that He will be at work and change our world. But sometimes prayer feels rather mysterious and we feel uncertain entering into it. If you want to know how to do something, ask an expert! I don't go to the doctor to get my car worked on or to a mechanic when I have a broken leg. Jesus had a vibrant prayer life with His father. His disciples saw Him spending the nights in prayer. Jesus was the expert "prayer warrior," and He took the time to teach His disciples—and us—how to pray. So, let's learn from the expert.

> Prayer changes us as we connect with God our Father.

Jesus' model for prayer

Jesus shared with us a guide for prayer that we call "The Lord's Prayer." While we often pray this prayer in church, it is not just for corporate worship. We can use this prayer as an outline for our own prayer life.

Looking at The Lord's Prayer (Matthew 6:9-13) we realize that our first priority is to praise and worship God. We pray to our Heavenly Father and worship Him as a Holy and Perfect God. We meditate on His wonders and use Scripture to describe the things that we love about Him.

As we are in awe of His character, we begin to pray that His will will be done. We begin to see how great His plans are. We want to see His Kingdom advance and to see Him establish His Lordship over all this earth, as it is in heaven.

He also wants us to pray about our physical, spiritual, and moral needs. We ask our caring God to meet our daily needs for food and provision. He also cares about our relationships and calls us to seek forgiveness for our sins, and also to forgive those who sin against us. He knows that we need to be in right relationship with Him and also with others. Lastly, He calls us to consider the way we live. We ask for His help in avoiding temptation and seeking deliverance from the evil one.

God desires to communicate with us both through His Word and prayer. He has given the Holy Spirit to help us understand His Word and to communicate with Him in prayer.

CONCLUSION

Getting to know God by spending time reading, meditating and memorizing the Bible and by taking time to pray are essential. We should set apart time every day to spend time with God in the Word and prayer. We also benefit from learning and sharing the Word of God with others and praying together as well.

Growing Through The Word And Prayer

7

IMPORTANT to Leader: Answers and notes to leaders are in gray, italicized text.

GOALS:

For a disciple to 1) understand the critical importance of the Word and prayer in the process of knowing God and doing His will. 2) understand the difference between interpretation and application. 3) have a time and place set aside to pray, read and study the Word.

GETTING STARTED:

What happens to a child who is malnourished, either because of the lack of food or the availability of the wrong food?

Physical growth is stunted, child is more susceptible to illness, may have vitamin and mineral deficiencies, bad eating habits are carried into adulthood, has weak bones and other physical problems, trouble learning, etc. A deprived child may interpret the situation as meaning that he isn't important.

Transition: We can also experience "spiritual malnutrition." In this lesson, we will learn about two sources of spiritual nourishment that significantly contribute to our spiritual development.

STUDYING TOGETHER:

THE WORD

Read II Timothy 3:16-17.

1. What does II Timothy 3:16-17 tell us about the source of God's Word?

    God gives the Word.

2. What role should Scripture play in the believer's life?

Read Psalm 1:1-6.

3. What habit does a blessed person follow both day and night?

    He reads (implied), studies (implied), and meditates on the law (Word) of God.

Read Psalm 19:7-11.

4. According to these verses, what might be some of the advantages of reading, studying, and meditating on God's Word?

   Revives the soul, makes us wise, gives us joy, helps us see the issues of life clearly, warns us of danger, gives great reward.

Like any other literature, a given passage in the Bible only has one meaning: the one intended by the author. (This is not to say that everyone agrees about the meaning.) While there can only be one meaning, there can be many applications of the truth.

Read Romans 12:18.

5. What is the one meaning of this passage?

   We are to do whatever we can to be in a peaceful relationship with everyone else.

6. What are some of the applications?

   I may need to go and ask forgiveness from someone. Or I may have to forgive someone. Or I may need to reach out to someone I've been ignoring, etc.

PRAYER

Read Matthew 7:7-8 and James 1:5, 4:8a.

7. What are some of the benefits of prayer?

   We receive what we ask for, we gain wisdom, we boldly come near to God, and He draws near to us, etc.

Read Matthew 6:9-13.

This prayer, the Lord's Prayer, is a model prayer for believers.

8. What are we instructed to do to focus on God in Matthew 6:9-10?

   Acknowledge Him as a Father (loving, protective, etc.). Worship His character (His name). Pray for the establishment and advancement of His Kingdom. Pray for His will to be accomplished on earth.

9. Matthew 6:11-13 focuses on the believer's needs. What needs does the prayer address?

   Our need for physical provisions. Our need for forgiveness. Our need for the power to resist evil.

LOOKING AT REAL LIFE:

10. Working as a group, list the "top 3" reasons disciples don't read, study, and meditate on God's Word on a regular basis.

    1. _____

    2. _____

    3. _____

11. Working as a group, list the "top 3" reasons disciples don't pray on a regular basis.

    1._____

    2._____

    3._____

12. Working from these lists, describe some ways to overcome these barriers.

    1._____

    2._____

    3._____

LOOKING AT MY LIFE:

If you have experienced blessings from prayer and personal Bible study in your life, share them with the group.

Think about the best time of day and the best place to have a regular habit of prayer and reading and studying the Word. Then, write down the specific time and place where you will do these two important activities each day this week.

Share your plan with one other person in your group. After sharing with one another, pray for each other that God would give both of you the discipline to begin and to continue these habits this week.

Transformation

We have long been fascinated by stories of transformation. Some of these are on the darker side, such as the monster Frankenstein who is cobbled together from old body parts and brought to life. The story of the pleasant, sociable Dr. Jekyll, who transforms into the evil, barbaric Mr. Hyde and then back again to Dr. Jekyll, has thrilled and frightened readers and movie goers alike. There are numerous variations in the man-turned-werewolf genre, but all feature some sort of gross transformation from man to wolf with fangs emerging, hair sprouting all over, clothes ripping off, and so on. Thankfully there are comedic versions of many of these horror stories, such as The Three Stooges' "We Want Our Mummy" and "Abbot and Costello Meet Frankenstein," so that even the faint-hearted among us can watch the show.

On the brighter, more uplifting side are such classics as Cinderella, which features the transformation of a lowly, unloved stepsister into a beautiful, beloved princess. In Beauty and the Beast, we see Belle transformed on the inside while the Beast is transformed outwardly. The Frog Prince, a Brothers Grimm fable, recounts the plight of a prince who has been turned into a frog by a wicked fairy. The reluctant kindness of a young princess breaks the spell and turns the frog back into a handsome prince again. Subsequently they are married and, of course, live happily ever after.

While we know that frogs do not actually turn into princes, they have a pretty remarkable transformation story of their own. They begin life as herbivorous tadpoles, with no legs and a tail. Remarkably, this tiny water-bound creature grows legs, loses its tail and becomes a carnivorous amphibian, typically within a matter of a few short weeks or months. Perhaps even more remarkable is the transformation of caterpillars into butterflies. The metamorphosis that takes a crawling caterpillar into a chrysalis and brings it out as a colorful, graceful butterfly is one of the most beautiful events in nature.

> Becoming a Christian is only the first step in the transformation process.

Christians, of all people, should know something about transformation. After all, Scripture makes it clear that God did not send His Son into this world only to save us but also to transform us. Twentieth-century pastor of Westminster Chapel in London, Martyn Lloyd-Jones, has rightly pointed out that, "Jesus demanded not a reformation of behavior, but a transformation of character." In fact, the goal of the Christian life is to be transformed into the likeness of Christ (Romans 8:29; II Corinthians 3:18).

Becoming a Christian is only the first step in the transformation process. When a person becomes a Christian, she immediately begins to be changed on the inside (II Corinthians 5:17) and is given everything she needs to continue to grow (II Peter 1:3). However, just as it is true in the physical world, so it is true in the spiritual world that growth takes time. Transformation is a life-long process which God will complete in each believer when Christ returns (Philippians 1:6).

While we have been given what we need to grow and God is committed to completing His work in our lives, we need to understand that transformation will not occur without intentional action on our part. However, we should have confidence that God can and will transform us if we apply three key concepts—know the Word, obey the Word, and experience the Word.

KNOW GOD'S WORD

Seminary professor and author Dr. Howard Hendricks has said, "The Bible was written not to satisfy your curiosity but to help you conform to Christ's image. Not to make you a smarter sinner but to make you like the Savior. Not to fill your head with a collection of biblical facts but to transform your life." This quote speaks to the importance of God's Word in the transformation process.

Even though, as noted above, new Christians have everything they need to grow, they are still newborn babes who need to be fed. Our primary source of nourishment is the Word of God. As the Apostle Peter put it in his letter to first-century Christians, "Like newborn babies, crave pure spiritual milk, so that by it you may grow up in your salvation." (I Peter 2:2) Knowing God's Word is the essential first step in the transformation process. If we do not know God's Word, then we will understand neither our new position in Christ nor the steps that we must take to grow in our Christian walk. In the absence of regular nourishment from God's Word, it is highly unusual for a new Christian to make significant progress.

Knowing God's Word is the essential first step in the transformation process.

Among the many ministries that the indwelling Holy Spirit performs in our lives is helping us to understand God's Word. The same Spirit who inspired the biblical writers now informs the biblical readers. While there may be many applications of any given Scripture passage (See Pocket Principle™ titled *Growing Through The Word And Prayer* in this series), there is only one correct interpretation. Therefore, we need to ask God the Holy Spirit to help us accurately understand the meaning of the passage at hand (I Corinthians 2:11-14). Without correct interpretation, there will not be effective application.

OBEY GOD'S WORD

The goal of the disciple is to apply and obey God's Word, not simply to hear and know it. We find in Scripture many exhortations to obedience. One of the classic passages is found in the letter of James, penned by the brother of Jesus. Early in his lengthy discourse on the relationship between faith and works, James writes that we must be doers of the Word and not hearers only (James 1:22-25). In this statement, James is merely echoing the words of Christ who repeatedly warned his audiences against listening but not obeying. In Matthew 7, Christ refers to the person who hears His words but does not put them into practice as a foolish man who builds his house on sand. When the storms of life come, that man's house and all of his hopes and dreams will come crashing down around him (Matthew 7:26-27). In another gospel account (John 8:31-32), Jesus tells His disciples that it is the one who holds to His teaching that is truly His disciple and will be set free (transformed) by the truth of His words. "Holding" implies much more than mental acknowledgement of the truth; rather, it implies putting the truth into practice in one's life.

Obedience (application of the Word) leads to blessings from God, both now and in eternity. We obey God and His Word because it is the right thing to do, not because of what obedience will do for us. However, God in His generosity has graciously built blessings into obedience. When we choose to obey God's Word, we bring Him glory by being His light in this world (Matthew 5:14-16) and we are promised reward for doing good (Galatians 6:9). We will be prosperous and successful in what really matters (Joshua 1:8). We will have a sure foundation, able to withstand the storms of life (Matthew 7:24-25). In the long run, we inherit eternal life (Romans 2:7,10) and eternal glory that will far outweigh any troubles we have experienced or sacrifices we have made in this life (II Corinthians 4:17).

> By "experience" we mean a person must live through a situation that verifies the truth.

We noted earlier that the Holy Spirit helps us to correctly interpret the meaning of Scripture. Now we are reminded that He also helps us to make application of the truth so that we might obey (Colossians 1:10-11). God living in us through the Holy Spirit knows us much better than we know ourselves. He knows what needs to happen in our lives for us to continue in our growth journey— pleasing God and bearing fruit. If we but seek and trust His guidance, He will lead us in the path of obedience that we are to follow.

EXPERIENCE GOD'S WORD

Although knowledge of God's Word and obedience to His Word are necessary for growth, they may not always be sufficient for real transformation to take place. We must acknowledge that sometimes believers get "stuck" in the transformation process. They find it hard to obey God's Word because they retain false beliefs that conflict with the truth. The "tapes" that play in their heads tell them one thing while God's Word tells them another. In these situations, it is necessary to correct the faulty belief system before such an individual can willfully and freely obey God.

To correct the faulty belief system and record new mental "tapes," the person must experience the truth rather than simply hear it. By "experience" we mean a person must live through a situation that verifies the truth. This process allows the person to own and to internalize the truth. Sometimes God orchestrates such situations Himself and, at other times, He wants the believer to help create the situation. The first action to take, in either case, is to identify the lie(s) that is creating the issue. After identifying the lie, a situation must be designed by the believer or he must be willing to enter into a situation that God or someone else has orchestrated. The situation must be one that will verify the truth. Ask God for wisdom in this process. Then ask God for courage as it is often necessary to take a risk in order to enter into such a situation. The risk may be that of embarrassment, of disappointment, of failure, or something else.

Jesus often put His disciples in situations where they could grow by experiencing the truth. Here is an example. Jesus knew that He was going to call some of His disciples to become His closest followers— to leave their nets and to go with Him wherever He went. He also knew that, at that point in His ministry, they had not yet embraced the truth of His ability to fully and completely provide for them. They were still relying on their own ability to catch fish and to provide for themselves, perhaps not acknowledging that even that ability was a gift from God. So early one morning, after the disciples had fished all night without success, Jesus instructed them to put down their nets in an area where they had been fishing without any results. In spite of their doubts, they obeyed by putting their nets back into the water. The result was a huge catch of fish! Because of their experience with the truth that Jesus could provide for them, they were able to trust Him and to leave life as they knew it and follow Him.

God, in His generosity, has graciously built blessings into obedience.

A common issue that many people struggle with is embracing the truth of God's unconditional love. If a person has not receive ample love in her life or has only received conditional love, telling that person over and over that God loves her is not likely to do much good. The person may give mental assent to the premise of God's love but not be able to feel it emotionally, and this divide sets up an internal conflict. Until this individual experiences true, unconditional love on a human level, she will have difficulty embracing it on a spiritual level. She needs to experience love in a new situation (other than the situation where she learned the lie). As she does so, new "tapes" will begin to play in her mind. Additional positive experiences with God and with others will reinforce belief in this new truth.

The role of the Holy Spirit and the importance of Christian community in this matter of experiencing truth cannot be over-emphasized. While truth can be experienced in isolation, that is probably more the exception than the rule. Small groups, or "cell groups" as they are known in many churches, provide an excellent forum for these types of experiences to take place. Others who know us well and are genuinely concerned for our spiritual well-being and growth can often be used by God to help us to identify wrong beliefs that are causing us problems. God will often use these same people in our lives to help us experience the reality of unconditional love, of forgiveness, and other truths we need to embrace.

CONCLUSION

The believer who is not regularly spending time in the Word will neither know it nor be likely to obey it. The believer who is not regularly spending time in healthy relationship with other believers will not experience truth in ways that may be necessary to overcome wrong beliefs. Therefore, we should make every effort to know, to obey, and to experience God's Word. These are keys to true transformation—to spiritual growth and blessing.

Transformation

GOALS:

For a disciple to understand that spiritual growth occurs when a person applies (obeys) the truth.

For a disciple to understand that spiritual growth occurs as lies (false beliefs) are replaced with truth.

For a disciple to understand that truth must be learned through experience.

GETTING STARTED:

Person A, through studying, is very knowledgeable about cars and how they work, and has also memorized the traffic laws. He has had one month of driving experience.

Person B has a general idea about how cars work and remembers many, but not all, of the traffic laws. He has driven a car for 10 years, has never been in an accident and has a reputation for being a good driver.

What are the pros and cons of each person's ability to drive a car? (Whom would you choose to ride with?)

Person A: Pros: May be able to fix a car, remembers all the traffic laws. Cons: Has little practical experience actually driving, driving a car isn't yet automatic to this person so must consciously think of every step.

Person B: Pros: Has proven he is a good driver in real life (no accidents and good reputation), is able to automatically do most of the things necessary to drive (put on brakes, turn corners, etc.). Has experience with many different driving situations. Cons: May not remember details of every traffic law, may not be able to diagnose and fix a car problem.

Transition: In the same way, experience with God's truth is essential to true transformation taking place.

STUDYING TOGETHER:

Read Matthew 7:24-27.

1. According to verse 24, Jesus said we would be wise if we did what?

    Hear His words (truth) and put the truth into practice.

2. According to verse 26, Jesus said we would be foolish if we did what?

    Hear His words (truth) and yet do not put the truth into practice.

3. In verse 25, what happens when the storms of life come against a person who has been applying truth in her life?

    She will not fall because she built on a solid foundation (applying God's truth).

4. In verses 26-27, what happens when the storms of life come against a person who has not been applying truth in her life?

    She will fall with a great crash because she built her house (life) on sand (not applying truth).

    Sometimes it is hard to obey God's Word. Why do you think this is true?

Read John 20:24-28.

5. A primary reason for disobedience to God's Word is that the believer has a competing belief system. In verse 25, what strongly held false belief did Thomas have?

    After the crucifixion and death of Jesus (which Thomas most likely witnessed or at least was well aware of), Thomas did not believe that Jesus had come back to life. We know this was a strong belief because he didn't believe in spite of the testimony of the other apostles who claimed to have seen Him.

Note to leader: Please be sure to make the following point: We all have some strongly held, false beliefs that have been internalized by our experiences.

6. Did just knowing the facts about Jesus' resurrection from his fellow apostles correct Thomas' false belief about Jesus? Why or why not?

   Intellectual knowledge alone will not correct his false belief. The experience of the crucifixion had most likely so impacted Thomas that the lie, that Jesus had not been resurrected, had already become deeply internalized in his mind.

7. What happened that helped Thomas replace his false belief about the resurrection? How did Thomas replace his false belief about the resurrection?

   He had a personal encounter with Jesus and actually touched the resurrected Jesus. Thomas experienced the truth and internalized it. Although Jesus will not materialize in bodily form to convince us of truth, He will make sure that we go through experiences that can help us internalize the truth and replace our false beliefs.

   Note to leader: *Please be sure to make the following point - We need to experience truth in order to internalize it and thus, have it replace our false beliefs.*

8. What do the following Scriptures indicate about how our experiences can help us internalize truth and grow spiritually?

   James 1:2-4—*We grow through the various trials in our lives.*

   Romans 5:3-5—*Suffering also produces growth in our lives.*

   Hebrews 12:10-11—*God disciplines us so we might grow spiritually.*

LOOKING AT REAL LIFE:

9. Lie: "God doesn't love me."

   Case Study: Jeremy is a believer in his mid 40s who has a wife and 2 children. When Jeremy was growing up, members of his family were critical, and they rarely showed their love to each other. Currently, he and his wife have communication difficulties, and Jeremy has trouble connecting with people. He often feels very alone. Intellectually he believes that God loves him, but emotionally he feels that God is distant and uncaring.

What kind of experience(s) do you think would help Jeremy really understand and internalize God's love?

Ideas:

* *Have a more mature believer at church develop a healthy trust relationship with Jeremy.*

* *Invite Jeremy to be in a men's group at church where there is open, honest communication about real life difficulties. In this group he can be open and honest about his life and then experience the groups' acceptance and unconditional love.*

LOOKING AT MY LIFE:

What is one spiritual truth that you've heard over and over, but still have a hard time internalizing and living out? (For example, the truth is that God uses trials in our lives because He loves us and wants us to grow to maturity. This truth may be a difficult one for you to grasp emotionally and live out.)

Close in a group prayer, thanking God that He is always at work seeking to make us like His Son, Jesus Christ. Pray that He will give each group member the strength and wisdom to apply truth this week.

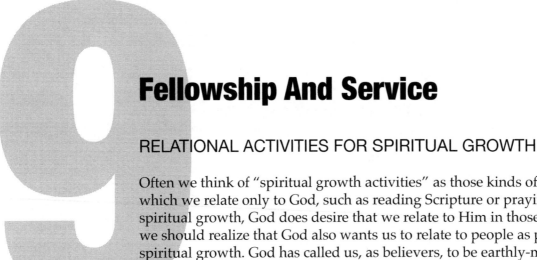

Fellowship And Service

RELATIONAL ACTIVITIES FOR SPIRITUAL GROWTH

Often we think of "spiritual growth activities" as those kinds of activities in which we relate only to God, such as reading Scripture or praying. As part of our spiritual growth, God does desire that we relate to Him in those ways. However, we should realize that God also wants us to relate to people as part of our spiritual growth. God has called us, as believers, to be earthly-minded as well as heavenly-minded. One of the ways that God wants us to be earthly-minded is by involving ourselves in significant relationships here on earth. God is a relational being and we, having been created in His image, are also relational beings.

There are many earthly activities that don't necessarily pertain to spiritual growth that are important to us, for example, getting an education or earning a living. And then there are other earthly activities, especially those that involve relating to others, that are essential to our spiritual growth. Two of those earthly relational activities are Fellowship and Service. Let us see what Scripture has to say about them and how it is that we grow spiritually by participating in them.

> God is a relational being and we, having been created in His image, are also relational beings.

Every summer for about 15 years, a group of seven to ten adults took a group of about 10 to 30 high school students on an amazing adventure. The stated purpose of the trip was to build houses for people in a small town in Mexico who lived in shacks put together with cardboard, mattresses, scrap lumber and wire. The group was going to serve those less fortunate than they were. The houses that were built every year by this group were no bigger than a tool shed. At the construction site, little Mexican children with bare, dusty feet ran around trying to help the "construction" workers. For some of the high school students, it was an eye-opening experience. Most of them had never seen such poverty. Many of them had never had an opportunity to serve in such a meaningful way, to meet such an obvious need for someone else. Since it was summer, the temperatures frequently were over 100 degrees. Without fail, even though these high school students would complain about heat not nearly as intense back home, they worked on under the hot Mexican sun. The joy of serving others had overcome any discomfort they might have. Even their lack of carpentry skills did not stop them from wanting to serve. Each one found a new skill or a different way that they could serve someone else.

One of the things that made the serving aspect so easy was the fellowship that happened among the people on the trip. After a two day van ride to Mexico, everyone had bonded in a special way. It makes for interesting interaction when people are that close together for that long. There was a lot of singing, sleeping, eating and game-playing on the van driving down. Then, when the work began in Mexico, the bonding continued. Added in to the fellowship mix were the people in Mexico. Usually a group of Mexican women would serve the Americans lunch every day. During this time of mutual serving, there was more singing, laughing and talking.

Frequently, some of the men from the neighborhood would join in and help out with the construction. And there were always groups of curious Mexican children hanging about. The day always ended at someone's house, sharing a meal with new Mexican friends, talking about the day and singing and praying together.

So, the stated purpose of the trip was to build houses for families that did not have them. However, the real purpose of the trip was to serve and be served and to love each other and enjoy interacting together. The fellowship and the service combined together to make the trip an unforgettable, life-changing experience for all involved. And in the process, God was glorified, since it was all done in His name.

FELLOWSHIP

What are some of the things that God, in Scripture, tells us about fellowship?

In I Corinthians 12:12-27, Paul talks about how a group of believers is called the "Body of Christ." This is a wonderful analogy as we think about how all of our own physical body parts work together. Just as our own body parts operate and are dependent on one another to function properly, so it is with the interaction and interdependence of people who are believers. In verses 11 and 12, Scripture says that God has arranged the body and all its parts exactly the way He wants them to be. Then, in Ephesians 4:11-16, Scripture says that the Body of Christ cannot reach maturity and maintain health without everyone in the body doing their part. We really need each other to flourish. In Romans 12:10-15, we learn that when one part of the Body suffers, the whole Body suffers; and when one part of the Body is honored, the whole Body is honored.

The author of Hebrews advises that we need to spend a significant amount of time with other members of the Body of Christ so that we can inspire one another to love and good works. This is found in Hebrews 10:24-25. When we are in fellowship with each other, we begin to care for each other. This in turn prepares us to care for unbelievers.

In Genesis 2:18, God states, "It is not good for the man to be alone." This is backed up by our own experiences. We usually know for ourselves that we don't function as well when we are isolated from other people. We each need a healthy support system. In Proverbs 13:20 and 27:17, we are told that it *does* matter who we spend time with. To create a healthy support system, we must select healthy people to be included in it.

There are many examples of fellowship. Often when we think of fellowship, we think of eating a meal together, or playing games with each other. Christian fellowship that fosters spiritual growth occurs whenever believers gather together and interact with each other. This could be in a worship service, a ball field, a Bible study, a pot-luck dinner, a walk in the park, etc. The goal of fellowship is for believers to spend time together and glorify and reflect God in whatever relational activity they engage in together.

Life on the road can be hard and discouraging. Yet it is not a journey we need undertake on our own. Part of God's gracious provision is fellow travelers along that road of faith. They are there to refresh us, to build us up, and to encourage us as we travel together to the New Jerusalem. Fellowship is not a luxury we can dispense with or should feel guilty about. It is a spiritual necessity vital to our spiritual growth. God has not created us to be alone but to exist and develop in relationship with others. Faith is nourished and supported in community.

Alister McGrath—The Journey: A Pilgrim in the Lands of the Spirit [1]

SERVICE

The second relational activity we will look at is service. Service can be defined as a good deed that we do for the benefit of another person, whether that person is a believer or an unbeliever. In Matthew 5:16, service is described as a way of "letting our light shine before others." Service to others includes helping someone with their physical needs, meeting someone's emotional needs, or ministering to someone's spiritual needs. When we give to the needs of others, we are participating in Service.

Jesus came to serve others and therefore, He is our model for serving. The greatest service that Jesus performed was when He gave His life for our salvation. Scripture says in Matthew 20:28 that Jesus, "the Son of Man did not come to be served, but to serve, and to give His life as a ransom for many." Throughout His ministry, Jesus was willing to take a humble position as He served others. A good example of this is found in John 13:1-5 where Jesus served His disciples by washing their feet. As we study Scripture and learn more about Jesus, we see that He calls us to follow His example of serving (see Matthew 20:25-28 and John 13:13-17).

> God uses the relational aspects of our lives to further our spiritual growth in Christ.

Our motive for serving others is our love for them. In I John 3:17-18, we are told that love generally manifests itself in some sort of outward deed. In our experience, we can usually attest to this. When we love somebody, we feel compelled to show some obvious external sign of that feeling. The kind of love that compels us to serve others also works as a testimony to God, showing the world that we belong to God. It is interesting how all this fits together. We serve because we love God and we love people; when we serve, we are being obedient to the teachings of Scripture; we feel good in our service, the person being helped benefits, and God is honored and receives glory. A win-win situation for all involved. These principles are described in Matthew 5:16 and in John 13:34-35. People will know we are followers of Christ by how we love.

As we grow spiritually by serving others, our capacity to help others grows. When we exercise our bodies, our muscles get stronger and we are able to do more advanced or strenuous exercise. Even young believers can encourage others by sharing their testimony of how they came to know Christ personally. So, sometimes we may serve others by simply encouraging them. Also as we grow and serve, we discover the spiritual gifts that God has given us. Scripture describes the spiritual gifts in I Corinthians 12:7-11. These gifts are given to us for the purpose of serving. As we grow in spiritual maturity, we become more sensitive to the voice of God as He directs us as we serve.

> Service can be defined as a good deed that we do for the benefit of another person.

An additional benefit of service is that God promises believers a reward for doing good deeds. In Romans 2:7,10, God speaks of and promises an eternal reward for our good deeds. In Galatians 6:9-10, we are promised an eventual good result, that is a "harvest," because of our good deeds if we remain faithful and persistent.

There are many types and ways of serving others. Some practical examples are doing something in secret for another person, doing small errands or daily tasks for another person, guarding the reputation of others, letting others serve us, practicing common courtesy, serving others through acts of hospitality, listening to others and bearing another's burdens. Sometimes we serve in large ways by lending our time and energy to a "service project" that helps meet the physical needs of another. Ways to serve are limitless and can be entered into daily and constantly.

As the cross is the sign of submission, so the towel is the sign of service. Service is not a list of things that we do, though in it we discover things to do. It is not a code of ethics but a way of living. The risen Christ beckons us to the ministry of the towel. Such a ministry, flowing out of the inner recesses of the heart, is life and joy and peace."

Richard Foster—Celebration of Discipline: The Path to Spiritual Growth [2]

CONCLUSION

Service and fellowship are closely connected because they are both relational activities. Frequently, they are practiced together. It is clear from Scripture that God uses these relational aspects of our lives to further our spiritual growth in Christ. As we move forward towards spiritual maturity, we are better able to impact our world for God.

End Notes:

(1) Alister McGrath, *The Journey: A Pilgrim in the Lands of the Spirit* (Doubleday, 1999), 112-113.

(2) Richard Foster, *Celebration of Discipline: The Path to Spiritual Growth* (HarperCollins Publishers, 1998), 126,134,140.

Fellowship And Service

IMPORTANT to Leader: Answers and notes to leaders are in gray, italicized text.

GOALS:

For a disciple to understand that being connected to the Body of Christ and serving others are both essentials for spiritual growth.

For a disciple to evaluate his present relationships in the Body and how he serves others.

GETTING STARTED:

What are the essentials needed to become a skilled tennis player?

Right equipment, a coach, location, partner(s), practice, a willingness to work hard, endurance…etc.

Transition: In the same way, there are essentials for spiritual growth. In this lesson we will look at two of these essentials: fellowship and service.

STUDYING TOGETHER:

FELLOWSHIP

Read I Corinthians 12:12-27.

1. In this passage Paul describes the church as a "body." What is the significance of the church being called the Body of Christ?

   It is interconnected, interdependent, living, diverse, dynamic.

2. What are some of the principles about the Body that Paul teaches in this passage?

   The key principles are:
   We all need each other.
   We all have value and are important.
   God is in charge, and He has arranged the body and its parts.
   All members of the body suffer if one suffers, and all rejoice if one is honored.

3. What do the following verses indicate about what our response should be as part of the Body of Christ?

   Hebrews 10:24-25—*We should meet together, encourage one another, and spur one another to love and good works.*

   Acts 2:42—*We should meet together for teaching, fellowship, prayer, eating together, and sharing communion.*

SERVICE

4. When you think about service, what comes to mind?

Read Matthew 5:16.

5. How does Matthew 5:16 describe "service"?

   Good deeds

6. What are some other good deeds you can think of?

Read Galatians 6:9-10.

7. According to these verses, whom should we serve?

   Believers and unbelievers

8. In Matthew 5:16 and Galatians 6:9-10, what kind of results will our good deeds bring?

   Light to the world, praise to God, will reap a harvest.

Leader: Be sure that group members understand that service can range from helping someone with physical needs, to meeting a person's psychological needs to ministering to his spiritual needs.

Read Matthew 20:25-28 and John 13:1-5,13-19.

9. What do these verses say about Jesus and His service?

    Jesus came to be a servant.
    He saved us by giving His life for our ransom.
    Jesus tells his disciples to do the same.
    Jesus humbly washed his disciples feet because He was confident of who He was and His destiny.
    Jesus gave us an example, and we are to follow it.

Read I John 3:17-18.

10. In these verses, John tells us that love for God (and others) should be our motive for serving others. What are some wrong motivations for serving?

    Trying to get something in return, trying to please God with good works, acting out of guilt or a sense of duty, etc.

LOOKING AT REAL LIFE:

11. What are some of the benefits of participating in the Body of Christ?

    Answers may be…learn about God, be equipped to do good works, have emotional and relational support, get help in times of need, receive godly counsel, be encouraged to do good works, etc.

12. What are some of the benefits to the server of serving others?

    Obedience to God, increased love for others, growing in "other-centeredness," feel good about yourself because you are having a positive impact on others and the world, etc.

LOOKING AT MY LIFE:

In your life, what opportunities do you have to participate in the Body of Christ and to serve others?

During this next week, how will you take advantage of these opportunities?

Understanding Our Enemies

The story is told of a reporter who was interviewing an old man on his 100th birthday. "What are you most proud of?" he asked. "Well," said the man, "I don't have an enemy in the world." "What a beautiful thought! How inspirational!" said the reporter. "Yep," added the centenarian, "I've outlived every last one of them."

Unfortunately for the Christian, no matter how long he lives there are enemies that will always be with him. Scripture identifies three such enemies—the world, the flesh, and the Devil. These enemies present constant challenges to the believer and can make spiritual growth more difficult. However, if we rise to the challenge, the difficulties we face with these enemies can also be a source of growth as we develop endurance and mature in godly character (James 1:2-4).

Experienced combatants tell us that the first rule in battle is to know the enemy. This lesson is designed to give the believer a better understanding of our enemies, thereby increasing our ability to defeat them and lessening their ability to hinder our spiritual growth. Our three primary enemies, as identified in Scripture, are described below.

THE WORLD

The first enemy that the believer must contend with is the world. By world, we do not mean the physical surroundings we inhabit. The most common use of the word "world" in the New Testament is that of an evil kingdom here on earth. It is a kingdom ruled by Satan (Ephesians 2:2) and populated by nonbelievers who are alienated from God and hostile toward Him (Colossians 1:21). When Christ comes back to earth to establish His eternal kingdom in all its fullness, this temporary evil kingdom will be done away.

When a person places her trust in Christ as Savior, she passes from death unto life, from the kingdom of darkness into the kingdom of light. Believers are no longer members of the worldly kingdom, but citizens of the kingdom of God (Colossians 1:13-14, 21-22). The Apostle Peter reminds us that we are foreigners and aliens here (I Peter 2:11).

Although believers are a part of God's kingdom, we must live in this evil world, and we are affected by it. Scripture tells us that this world system is characterized by the lust for physical pleasure, the lust for everything we see, and pride in possessions (I John 2:15-17). Or as author Charles Swindoll puts it in *Living Above the Level of Mediocrity*, "The world system is committed to at least four major objectives, which I can summarize in four words: fortune, fame, power, and pleasure."

We are surrounded by unbelievers whose lives are driven by these objectives, yet, as citizens of the heavenly kingdom, we must stand firm and resist the temptation to be swept along by the current. The result is that we are mistreated and persecuted for our values and beliefs, sometimes purposely and sometimes inadvertently. Sometimes this opposition will take the form of ridicule, sometimes of outright hostility. Sometimes we just have to deal with the subtle, lonely feeling that we are out of place here and do not belong. And, of course, there is the ever-present pain of living in a fallen world, characterized by unhealthy relationships, harmful behaviors, and other consequences of sin.

In I John 2:15-17 we (believers) are told to defend ourselves from the world by not loving it. What does this mean? One way to not love the world is to focus on loving and following God. Keeping our focus on God and His will enables us to maintain our priorities and stand firm in the face of opposition from the world. A second way to defend ourselves is to remove ourselves from tempting or hurtful situations. The Holy Spirit empowers us to discern when a particular situation is beyond our ability (as believers) to withstand, acknowledging that withdrawal from the situation is the wisest defensive action. A third defensive is to not take our guidance/direction from the world. Instead, the believer's guidance must come from God's Word, the Holy Spirit and the wise counsel of other believers.

Some believers have misunderstood what our stance should be regarding the earthly kingdom in which we live. They think that the only way to be true to God is to live apart from this world as much as possible. They try to avoid contact or relationships with unbelievers, and they often criticize other believers whom they consider to be compromising with the world. Interestingly, Jesus faced similar criticism from the religious leaders of His day. As children of God and members of His eternal kingdom, we have a responsibility to be a positive influence in the midst of the people about us. We are not to let the world influence us toward evil, but rather we are to be God's ambassadors and influence this world for Him.

> This sin nature is more than just wrong thinking or bad habits. It is an inner bent and set of desires that influence us to oppose God.

THE FLESH

The second enemy of the Christian is the flesh. Some years ago, a cartoon strip named Pogo featured the character of that name surrounded by pollution and destruction. Pogo is seen remarking to his sidekick, "We have met the enemy and he is us." Indeed, just as we humans have done much to pollute and trash God's creation, so we have a sin nature that continues to pollute and corrupt God's new creation in us. The enemy lives within.

All humans are born with a sin nature. This sin nature is more than just wrong thinking or bad habits. It is an inner bent and set of desires that influence us to oppose God and His righteousness. J. Oswald Sanders, a noted Christian author, wrote in his book *Enjoying Intimacy with God* that the flesh is "the evil principle in man's nature, the traitor within who is in league with the attackers without. The flesh provides the tinder on which the devil's temptations can kindle." James, the brother of Jesus, describes the influence of our flesh when he writes that we sin when we are lead astray by our own lusts (James 1:14).

The unbeliever is controlled by this sin nature. The Christian still has the sin nature residing within, and must battle against it until the sin nature ceases to exist at death. Although the Christian still has to contend with the sin nature, he has become a new creation in Christ and has been given the gift of the Holy Spirit. Through the power of the indwelling Spirit, we can overcome the sin nature at any given moment in time. In fact, it is impossible to yield to the flesh or sin nature at the same time that we are yielded to the Spirit of God, since the two are contrary to one another. "Walk in the Spirit, and you shall not fulfill the lust of the flesh," writes the Apostle Paul in Galatians 5:16 (*New King James*). And he affirms confidently in Romans 8:12, "You have no obligation whatsoever to do what your sinful nature urges you to do." (*New Living Translation*)

> One way not to love the world is to focus on loving and following God.

Just as believers are given defenses against the world, we have been given defenses against the influence of the sin nature (in each one of us). Scripture tells us that the believer can defend herself against the flesh and overcome the sin nature at any given moment through the power of the Holy Spirit (Galatians 5:16; Romans 8:13). Because the sin nature remains active in the believer until she physically dies, the battle with the sin nature continues throughout life. For this reason, it is essential that a believer (a new believer or a mature believer) remain alert and filled with the Spirit.

THE DEVIL

Our third enemy is the Devil. Far from being a cartoon character with little horns and a pitchfork, the Devil is a real enemy, a dangerous enemy, and one that seeks to cause us harm. Scripture warns that the Devil goes about looking to catch Christians off guard so he can destroy them. The Devil and the army of evil spirits at his command in the invisible realm hate Christians because we have cast our allegiance with his archenemy. Once a high-ranking angel in God's kingdom, the Devil chose to rebel against God. Now he is the embodiment of evil and opposes God and everything He stands for.

In keeping with His perfect purposes, God, who is all-powerful, is allowing the Devil to have limited authority for a season. The Devil and all his helpers will eventually be rendered powerless, and he will be thrown into a lake of fire where he will be tormented forever. The final chapter in the story has already been written, so the Christian does not need to worry who will win out in the end.

In the meantime, however, the believer must contend with this enemy. He must stay on guard and recognize when the Devil is on the attack. Far from being helpless against the strategies and attacks of the Devil, the believer has the power to resist him. Peter wrote that we should stand firm against the Devil (I Peter 5:8-9). In fact, James wrote to the early believers, "Resist the Devil, and he will flee from you." (James 4:7) And in his letter to the Christians in Ephesus, the Apostle Paul goes into detail regarding the equipment that we have been given to fight our enemies (Ephesians 6:13-18). He states specifically that this armor and these weapons, such as the belt of truth, the breastplate of righteousness, the shield of faith, and the sword of the Spirit, have been given to us so that we can "take our stand against the devil's schemes."

> God, who is all-powerful, is allowing the Devil to have limited authority for a season.

One of the Devil's favorite tactics is to try to create doubt in the mind of Christians. Satan is known as the father of lies (John 8:44), and he is a master at distorting the truth. This has been his approach from the beginning. His method with Eve was to distort the truth and create doubt in her mind about the goodness of God. He exercises the same tactic with believers today. And, if we listen to the Devil's lies and allow unfavorable circumstances to sway our opinion, we can find ourselves doubting the goodness or power of God. It is imperative that we immerse ourselves in God's Word and arm ourselves with His truth and use prayer to separate God's truth from the enemy's lies.

The words of *A Mighty Fortress Is Our God*, an old Christian hymn written by the reformer Martin Luther in the sixteenth century, continue to encourage twenty-first century believers as we battle the Devil. Excerpts from the first and third verses read as follows: "For still our ancient foe, does seek to work us woe, his craft and power are great, and armed with cruel hate, on earth is not his equal. And though this world with devils filled, should threaten to undo us, we will not fear for God has willed His truth to triumph through us. The prince of darkness grim, we tremble not for him, his rage we can endure. For lo, his doom is sure. One little word shall fell him." In these verses we are reminded of the power of the enemy yet, more importantly, of the victory we have through Jesus Christ.

CONCLUSION—MORE THAN CONQUERORS

An important part of spiritual growth is learning to overcome our enemies in this life. The believer must be aware of her enemies and make use of the weapons mentioned in Scripture to combat these enemies. As we engage in battle, we rest secure in the promises of God's Word. In the eighth chapter of Romans, Paul asks rhetorically, "If God is for us, who can be against us?" After listing several things that could potentially defeat us, Paul states emphatically that we are more than conquerors through Christ Jesus (Romans 8:34). He then goes on to affirm that nothing in all creation is able to separate us from the love of God through Christ Jesus our Lord (Romans 8:39).

Understanding Our Enemies

10

GOAL:

For a disciple to acknowledge that in the Christian life there are difficulties because we have enemies and to begin to identify how these enemies presently affect her.

GETTING STARTED:

As a teenager, which of the following was the greatest battle you faced?

☐ battle for good grades

☐ battle for popularity

☐ battle against your parents

☐ battle with your siblings

☐ other: _____

Transition: In today's lesson, we will study another kind of battle. As Christians we encounter three enemies that battle against us.

STUDYING TOGETHER & LOOKING AT REAL LIFE:

Read Ephesians 2:1-3.

1. Using Ephesians 2:1-3 as a basis, define the following enemies that work together and battle against us in the Christian life:

    *   World—*an evil kingdom here on earth whose ways lead to disobedience; this "world" is ruled by Satan and populated by non-believers who are alienated from and hostile to God (Colossians 1:21; Romans 8:7).*

    *   Flesh—*the "flesh" is often translated in the New Testament as the "sin nature"; its desires and thoughts influence non-believers against God; the flesh also creates a conflict within believers that opposes the positive influence of the Holy Spirit (Galatians 5:16-17).*

- Devil—*the devil is the embodiment of evil who opposes God and everything He stands for; he is the leader of an army of evil spirits in the invisible realm ("the ruler of the kingdom of the air"); God is all-powerful and is allowing the Devil to have limited authority for a season (Ephesians 6:10-12).*

2. In His Word God tells us about defenses to use against each of these enemies:

   - World—**Read I John 2:15-17.** What does it mean to "not love the world"?

     Not taking our direction or guidance from the world; removing self from tempting or hurtful situations, focusing on loving and following God.

   Have you known people who have been wounded or damaged by this evil world in any of the following ways: addictions, unhealthy relationships, persecution, feelings of shame, lies and distortions of the truth? Share one example with the group.

   - Flesh—**Read Galatians 5:16-23.** How does living by the Spirit overcome the acts of the sinful nature (flesh)?

     The Spirit provides power for obedience, gives new desires, produces the fruit of the Spirit that counteract the acts of the sinful nature.

   - Devil—**Read James 4:7.** How does a Christian resist the Devil?

     Through prayer (Matthew 4), by rebuking Satan in the name of Christ, by using scripture to counter his lies and deceptions.

3. In **John 16:33,** what assurance did Jesus give us about the battle against our enemies?

   The war will be won and we can have peace in the midst of our difficulties because of what God has done in Christ.

LOOKING AT MY LIFE:

Which of the three enemies that we face—the world, the flesh, and the Devil—do you think that you have been least able to recognize in your life?

Which of these three enemies do you sense is battling the strongest in your life right now? Join with another person and pray for God's strength to help you overcome this enemy this week.

What's Next?

We hope you enjoyed this study.
You may be wondering: "So, what's next?"
I'm glad you asked.

If your group has benefited from their experience with this study, we suggest that if you have not studied *Knowing God* and *Understanding People*, you study them. If you have completed all of the Cornerstone series, continue studying topics in Phase III (Positional Truth, Healthy Relationships, Ministry Principles, Spiritual Warfare, Inductive Bible Study, and others). (See link on next page.)

Because you have chosen to lead, we want to do all we can to support you. In addition to the materials provided in this workbook, we would like to also offer you a free download of the Teaching Outlines for *Growing Spiritually*. (See link on next page.)

If you want to study materials that will help you grow as a leader, you might be interested in the *Small Groups Manual* (WDA) or the *Life Coaching Manual* (WDA), both can be found on the WDA store at www.disciplebuilding.org. (See link on next page.)

Also, **on the WDA website you will find explanations about the meaning of the different Phases I through V.** If you want to understand more about progressive growth there is a free download on our website called *Disciple Building: A Biblical Framework*. This explains the biblical basis for our disciple building process. (See links on next page.)

If you want to understand more about the Restorative Ministry, there is a free download entitled *How Emotional Problems Develop* on our website. The Restorative Ministry addresses relational and emotional needs that affect a disciple's ability to grow spiritually. (See links on next page.)

We look forward to a long association with you as you seek and follow our Lord, and grow in Christ using WDA Materials.

Bob Dukes

Knowing God, Understanding People and *Growing Spiritually:*

www.disciplebuilding.org/product-category/laying-foundations-phase-2

Phase III: Equipping for Ministry:

http://www.disciplebuilding.org/product-category/equipping-for-ministry-phase-3

Free Teaching Outlines for *Growing Spiritually:*

http://www.disciplebuilding.org/materials/growing-spiritually-teaching-outlines-free-download

Small Groups Manual and *Life Coaching Manual:*

www.disciplebuilding.org/materials/description_materials/4

www.disciplebuilding.org/product-category/leadership-manuals

Meaning of Phases I-V:

www.disciplebuilding.org/about/phases-of-christian-growth/2

Free Download of *Disciple Building: A Biblical Framework:*

www.disciplebuilding.org/store/leadership-manuals/disciple-building-a-biblical-framework

Free Download of *How Emotional Problems Develop:*

www.disciplebuilding.org/store/leadership-manuals/how-emotional-problems-develop

About the Restorative Ministry:

www.disciplebuilding.org/ministries/restorative-ministry

About WDA

WDA's mission is to serve the church worldwide by developing Christlike character in people and equipping them to disciple others according to the pattern Jesus used to train His disciples.

Organized as Worldwide Discipleship Association (WDA) in 1974, we are based in the United States and have ministries and partners throughout the world. WDA is a 501c(3) non-profit organization funded primarily by the tax-deductible gifts of those who share our commitment to biblical disciple building.

WDA is committed to intentional, progressive discipleship. We offer a flexible, transferable approach that is based on the ministry and methods of Jesus, the Master Disciple Builder. By studying Jesus' ministry, WDA discovered five phases of Christian growth. The Cornerstone series focuses on the first and second phases, Phase I: Establishing Faith and Phase II: Laying Foundations (*Knowing God, Understanding People* and *Growing Spiritually*). This series addresses the needs of a young believer or a more mature believer who wants a review of foundational Christian truths.

The remaining phases are: Phase III: Equipping for Ministry; Phase IV: Developing New Leaders and Phase V: Developing Mature Leaders.

For more information about WDA please visit our website: www.disciplebuilding.org.

If you are interested in seeing other WDA materials, please visit the WDA store: www.disciplebuilding.org/store.

WDA Partnerships

Help us build disciples worldwide.

You can help us fulfill the great commission by becoming a Worldwide Discipleship Association (WDA) partner. WDA's mission is to serve the church worldwide by developing Christlike character in people and equipping them to disciple others according to the pattern Jesus used to train His disciples.

Since our inception in 1974 our materials and processes have been used in more than 90 U.S. cities and in over **55 countries**. We have created **over a million direct discipleship impacts** and have conducted face-to-face **training to over 17,000 pastors and leaders** around the globe! **Your support of WDA is vital to the success of our mission.** We pledge to serve as faithful stewards of your generous gifts to the ministry.

www.disciplebuilding.org/give/wda-partnership

Become a Partner Today

38400022R00060